Trauma Recovery Manual

By

gregory david

ISBN: 9798759715252

Gratitude & respect to the wonderful sculptor Josie Spencer www.josiespencer.com for the cover picture of one of her magnificent creations.

Cover design by Scott Gaunt Designs:
scottgaunt@hotmail.co.uk

Trauma Recovery Manual

(navigation to authentic you)

Dedicated to my Angels:

Trisha, Katherine, (Mr.) Malik aka 'The Don', The Croyde (Trust) Brothers, tenacious Andy, inspirational William.

*A massive thank you to the SurvivorsUK crew and all the brothers that sail aboard. A shout out to; ASCA, 'OneinFour', HAVOCA, NAPAC, Humen, Momentum(Devon), Onroad media, The Next Step Counseling (Mike & Thom), and all those providing support to survivors.

To my love, Heather (…the spell you cast on me when we were six….I am so lucky…)

** Disclaimer: the above mentioned organizations are not necessarily advocates of, or therefore support, any of the views expressed in this book.*

Preface

This is the book I needed in October 2015 when my nervous breakdown really took hold, when I was desperate. It is a straight talking ‘how to’, providing tools you can *choose* to get you through your journey and past your distress. It won’t give you all the answers and some of the stuff won’t suit you. A phrase I learnt from group therapy, ‘take the positives and leave the rest behind’.

I could be wrong (I now acknowledge I can be which is a new concept i.e. being right was a defense and safety) but I recall reading, humankind’s knowledge of everything; the Earth, nature, the laws of physics, the Oceans, the cosmos, history, etc, could be measured at unit 1 in 1955. I remember that, coincidentally, by 1975 that unit was 25. By the 90’s, when the digital age was embryonic, it had moved to 195. Our knowledge is soaring exponentially and knowledge about us, the human being, is accelerating too.

There are estimates there are up to 10 million undiscovered species in our Oceans. We’ve recently discovered the planets in the solar system have immensely complex ecosystems; several moons have water, and let’s face it that’s just the back yard!

Similarly, the MRI scanner introduced us with more clarity to the previously speculated upon but mostly unknown frontier of the human brain, bringing new data on how the most complex organ on the planet operates and how it is affected by trauma.

We don't know much. Any individual knows only a minute fraction of all we have learnt. So, what about what we don't know we don't know?

I know what I know. I have endured a life of silent mental illness, of struggles with depression, addiction, imposter syndrome, fear, anxiety, grandiosity, paranoia…eventually the elastic snapped and I endured a crippling mental breakdown. I often longed to kill myself and nearly did several times. I recovered. Now I'm not an addict, and I want to live, I love every day and love being me. This book is how I did it.

Note: I endured repeated trauma as a child (labeled CPTSD: complex post traumatic stress disorder). The trauma caused my mental illness. By way of recovery I didn't only deal with the symptoms e.g. depression. I dealt with the cause i.e. having been traumatized.

The cause of the trauma/CPTSD: CSA (childhood sexual abuse).

This isn't a book by an academic with a qualification in psychology. It is how to build a shelter, get some food, light a fire, signal for and get help, by someone who has! It is a manual for survival and recovery from trauma and mental health conditions.

And know this: the book isn't a quick fix medication or *just* positive affirmations and meditation.

Let's be clear: recovery takes work. I mean, at times getting out of bed early on a dark, cold, wet Monday morning and doing something you don't want to do work. This is what worked and works for me.

If I slept after always self medicating heavily, I would often wake up thinking 'oh no, I'm still alive and I've got to spend the whole day being me. Is this the day I finally make the decision to commit suicide and end the misery of being me?'

Now, I am grateful to be alive and welcome everyday. I know that feeling will never leave me.

The following should be useful to most of us at some point in our often demanding and overwhelming lives. You will be challenged to examine the cause of your negative behaviors i.e. the source of your emotional distress, providing tools to aid your journey of change and recovery. Moreover, it guides you in healing the cause of the wound rather than only applying a remedy to the symptoms.

Know this: your journey is your journey – no one else's. This feels lonely but you will find the opposite once you speak out. You will detect all sorts of tools, methods and books that suit you, and discover a natural ability to discern what is right for you. You will uncover a 'something' in your nature, your intuition perhaps, guiding you and ensuring you float to the surface. And moreover, be certain, you will make connections with other people like never before.

In the early stages of dealing with trauma you may be in a desperate state, ready to try and believe anything. Paradoxically, the time you most need help is when you are most vulnerable therefore open to exploitation and 'stinking thinking', so you may find yourself 'clutching at straws'. Instead, step back and move in a slow measured fashion. ***There is no quick fix.***

This book is meant to be ingested as a whole. It is not 'do this now and move on to the next stage, then do that and then do this…'. It does not provide a linear path; reading is, so I am hamstrung by having a start and end point. I'd rather transmit what I have to say in a picture, enabling you to view my offering in its entirety and focus on parts that suit, if at all. But via the written word it is, as such I invite you to treat it as a whole entity rather than a flat pack construction plan. And I stress: your journey is your journey. It is different to mine but contrarily, the same; you'll get what I mean my beautiful sister and equally, you too my beautiful brother.

Prologue

Delhi in 1987: at the end of two years of traveling around Asia and India I checked into a hostel. I paid a week in advance for a solitary hut on the roof. I'd been feeling unwell but this was not unusual given my diet. I recall the conscious thought of nobody having any idea where I was, not having contacted any friends or dysfunctional family members for way over three years, having prior to my journey been living in Japan for a year, and Australia before that.

I began to convulse. Okay, I am ill. I vomited, dry wretched and my bowels cramped. Shortly, I was shitting and puking as good as simultaneously. I stripped naked then oscillated between sitting on and kneeling over this filthy toilet until I had only the strength to lie curled around it and convulse involuntarily without any discharge from either end making into the bowl, all just splattering around me.

This went on for four days. That is four whole days and nights lying next to a toilet getting weaker and weaker, by now just cramping out bile.

It felt like the devil had manifested itself as a giant which had me clenched in both hands and was wringing me. For a while I actually begged silently for mercy. I have never begged for mercy. The devil twisted and twisted unrelentingly. It would stop and wait, give false hope, then twist again, and when the pain was excruciating it would twist some more, and just when I could not bear it any longer it would hold tight and keep me twisted.

I have looked death in the face a couple of times given that I am the risk taking variety of trauma survivors but this was different because previously they were usually heart stopping moments, whereas this confrontation was elongated.

I went through various phases psychologically. Panic was the first. Panic because my reality had changed so dramatically I couldn't accept it or, seemingly, do anything about it. Three days in I began to believe I might actually die in this hut on this roof in this 'bathroom'.

I recall I spent sometime hallucinating. The same vision I have tried to cultivate in your mind of a giant holding me was the actual vision I was facing.

But there were gaps between the unpredictable twists. In those gaps I ***decided*** to think. You see, part of the problem I had was coming to terms with the fact that nobody was going to appear and help me. No one was going to come and knock on the door. This was not a room service kind of place. I was on my own. So what was I going to do about my situation?

The first thing I decided was to ***decide*** I was going to survive.

You see, I did have choices. I could decide to resign myself to dying and let go, and with that, deplete my will. Or, I could not want to die but expend energy by indulging in panic, questioning and worrying.

I didn't do either because I accepted the situation is as it is. I decided to give myself the best chance of getting through which, logically, was to decide I was going to survive. So, I decided to tell myself that at some point it would pass, the twists would weaken and I would get through it. I painted a picture in my mind of getting up off the floor and finding the strength from somewhere to get down the stairs and get help.

Once I made this decision I didn't go back on it. I decided to stick with this decision. It was a good one: the best one. The major physical benefit being that I didn't waste any energy panicking, and it is likely there were spiritual benefits aiding my recovery.

Then I made a major ***pragmatic*** choice fairly early on. I maneuvered my body as best I could so my mouth was not slumped near the floor, and with the back of my hand wiped away the puke so as not to intoxicate myself with the fumes (see Jimi Hendrix cause of death) if I should fall asleep/unconscious.

Then I decided to breathe deeply whenever possible. I decided to relax my body: conserve any strength I may have. In parallel, I decided to view this as a challenge, see how much I could take. Plus, find out just how much this giant devil could dish out, and I *decided* I would take more than it would give.

Even sometime after the whole event having further traveled back through Thailand (including being, fortunately, physically dragged away from an opium den on the Burmese border just before addiction sunk its teeth into me) where I found a café that served beans on toast (my staple), but despite this on meeting my mate on my return to Sydney his face dropped.

"Sheit mayt, wih gohdah gitsem Aussie tuhkah ensyde jah."

Twenty eight years later aged 53 lying in bed in our flat in London one morning someway into the early stages of my breakdown, I found myself shaking and unable to talk. My wife was hurriedly getting ready for work but sensed something was wrong; I managed to put her off. Whatever was coming up I needed to be alone and go through it, anticipating her angst would not help.

The shivers turned into convulsions. I felt a gagging sensation. Memories were flashing back. I knelt naked over the toilet bowl and dry wretched. I began to sob. I wailed out hopelessness as I convulsed and gagged and my insides tried to squeeze up my dry throat. I coughed and gagged and coughed so violently, and then,…. what, what was happening? Joining the physical, mental and emotional hurricane of turmoil, splat, splat, splat, splat, cough after cough after choking cough. I was coughing blood. The toilet bowl, the edge and the lifted lid, were getting covered in blood. Splat, splat, splat, splat, splat, unstoppable, bright red blood, a lot of, splat, splat, splat, my, splat, bright, splat, red, splat, blood, splat.

I actualized re-experiencing being abused by my own father in the early hours of the morning as a small boy: when I used to vomit by the bed. The memories were erupting from my body into my mind, and the convulsions were so powerful I had ripped and internal organ and was about to bleed to death.

My mind was racing down avenues, I would later explore in depth, as it wrestled desperately with the concept I was sexually abused by my own father: my childhood had been a lie; utterly cheated of my childhood. I was assaulted with pure cruelty, a myriad of thoughts fused with the total terror of being a small defenseless boy, this huge dark figure, the weight suffocating me; all whilst trying to grasp the reality of staring not more than a foot away from a toilet bowl being splattered by blood, my blood I was coughing up. Now I was going to die. The hopeless injustice of dying like this was one of the many thoughts and feelings I had balanced against my long held belief that I was different, an outsider, perhaps inherently evil and knew the powers that be, I knew nothing of, needed to take me this way. I had to go. I deserved to die for whatever I had done so wrong in this life, or perhaps the last, or that some need to die from injustice and I was one.

But I had been here before. Survival is first and foremost about ***making the decision*** to survive.

I made it to A&E (fortunately, there was a hospital within walking distance) to be told I had ripped my throat rather than an internal organ. Even so, I don't remember ever hearing of anyone coughing and choking so violently they tore their throat.

This event was the beginning of the Tsunami that was my breakdown, and my subsequent Odyssey to recovery from complex post traumatic stress disorder (CPTSD).

Recovery has taken considerably more than beans on toast and Aussie tucka. I am going to explain how I did it, albeit in essence I already have!

Three things.

1. ***You*** make the decision.
2. Do something about it.
3. …errr….is going to take more explaining…….(*see below*)…

Contents

Part A – Introduction

1. Mental (& Emotional) Health

My uncle died in a 'mental institution'. I believe he had been diagnosed as a paranoid schizophrenic. I *think* I know what that is, so I probably don't!

As I write I have a sinking feeling of treachery. We didn't talk about Uncle John. The subject of 'Uncle John' was taboo. Why? Bottom line: Uncle John represented shame. The shame of Uncle John's mental illness reflected *badly on the family*. Uncle John spending most of his life in and out of The Towers Hospital was rarely mentioned.

'The Towers' *was* referred to as the 'nut house' or 'the loony bin' back in my youth.

Uncle John was dark and dangerous and talking about him, even in hushed tones, brought darkness and danger.

For someone to be labeled 'mentally ill' was a forever curse. They were a social leper. They had the plague – keep away - any talk of the mentally ill would reflect badly on you and somehow associate you with mental illness, so you too would be infected and become a pariah, an outcast.

Uncle John came along to my wedding 'do'. I got married to my childhood sweetheart in Kenya and had a 'do' later in our home town. I recall in all the hubbub of the arrangements speaking out and getting an invite to him. I remember he approached with his gift he had obviously given a lot of thought. We chatted. I could see love and respect in his eyes.

He was so glad to be at the 'do', that he was involved. I could sense him trying his very best to be the best he could be; humble, pleasant, polite, listening, taking interest, desperate to give a good account of himself, to be accepted.

Uncle John was a lovely man. He had a beautiful soul, I saw it.

We all get physically ill. Sometimes, as we pass through life, we nearly all get mentally ill.

We need to scrap our previous prejudice towards mental illness. We are now, at last, doing a good job of working towards just that. Speaking out about mental illness is becoming acceptable. I suspect, without reflecting cynicism, it is becoming fashionable to do so among 'the stars'; similar to talking about addiction which, in balance, helps to normalize it i.e. makes it okay for the rest of us to sound out our troubles. I am in favour of celebrities voicing their troubles, even if by way of self promotion, looking for lucrative limelight (an addiction in itself?). Hey, whatever it takes to get rid of the stigma and enable people to feel comfortable speaking out!

Men especially are not so open to speaking out. Suicide among males is an indicator of this *(men are 3 times more likely to die by suicide than women).*

I wonder if we should re-brand 'mental illness', without diluting its significance. Call it something else perhaps? Use another phrase that doesn't make us uncomfortably silent? Stop us choosing to avoid that person with that 'label'.

Why is it okay to talk about physical illness but not mental illness? Why does it have a stigma?

At least one in four of us endure a mental health issue at some point in our life. It's not rare…so that's not the reason we shun it.

Do we feel talking about 'it' will somehow infect the image we hope to project? Like my family?

Are we designed to deal with the speed and complexity of current daily life which appears to be getting more complicated and, as such, perhaps there is a correlation with the rise in mental illness given, for example, the alarming statistics on self harm?

And consider this: one in four female and one in six male minors are sexually abused. Sexual abuse causes trauma, and trauma causes mental health issues, as does physical abuse, neglect and psychological abuse of children. Even if you weren't abused, you'll know someone who was, even if they don't declare it (it's most unlikely they will – again, stigma).

Mental health is a concern for all of us.

You will possibly endure some trauma in your life.
Having a mental health issue, or issues, is 'normal' (like the ad' says – there are 7 billion different types of 'normal').

You're not alone, far from it. In fact, that's a significant problem …..resource….resource to deal with the scale of the issue.

Finding and maintaining mental and emotional health ought to be a significant part of your life. It's down to you to make the first move. If you desire emotional and mental health you can do it. You can do it for you, but a big, big part of doing it for you is reaching out and sharing: taking the risk.

Life ***is*** short. How you go through it ***is*** up to you – no one else. It ***is*** your choice and you ***do*** have a choice, no matter where you are at right at this moment.

2. Philosophy of Recovery

I'll transmit certainty up front. The certainty I know you may crave which I am qualified to give, that I needed and sometimes received. The certainty I give you right now is your potential to recover. It is 'doable' no matter what state you are in, no matter your background, no matter what happened to you. But how you apply the tools, ideas and concepts if at all, is your choice.

You may be ready to accept you have an issue. Acknowledgement is the first step. Depression may be a symptom of trauma, if it exists, and you may have yet to link them. I hadn't made the connection when I finally sought help, I just felt depressed. Few make the association. Why? One viable reason: the medical profession is only just beginning to accept that trauma (especially childhood trauma) is a primary cause of mental health issues, as such, people don't receive the depth of guidance and help required. The healthcare frontline may only offer psychotropic medication in part because it's easier i.e. they don't have the time and resource to address your situation. And they don't ***fully*** realize and accept past/childhood trauma ***directly*** affects a person's *current* emotional and mental state. I know this from first hand experience affirmed by other trauma survivors, and confirmed for me by a booklet circulated to GP's of stories by survivors of CSA who were ex-addicts, which I contributed to; its purpose to express the association between childhood abuse (CA) and addiction. It was designed to educate them, as in it being a new concept to them!

I also suspect that less than a majority of counselors and therapists look for abuse in the childhood of their clients, despite the conclusive extensive evidence that CA and mental health issues are directly linked. This may be unfair. My comment is based on my own experience and that of other survivors that have been involved in 'educating' therapists in relation to CA and mental health issues.

I am biased in the belief that if abuse exists in childhood it is a primary cause of mental health issues rather than just a contributory factor.

You may not have experienced sexual, physical, psychological, or neglect in childhood, I am certainly not trying to put it there. You may have endured a traumatic experience/s in adulthood and you either know, or wonder, if this is manifesting in mental and emotional health issues. Or there is no trauma, either way you will gain a lot by reading on.

The trauma caused by childhood abuse affects deeply. It is proven CA molds brain development, the neural pathways. CA changes the chemical balance in the brain. This becomes about Cortisol, the Hypothalamus, the prefrontal cortex, and other complex stuff I have read about but never managed to assimilate (but don't let that stop you). Childhood abuse affects the child's development into adolescence and adulthood, on every level; physically, spiritually, emotionally and mentally.

I am recovering from CSA. I am recovering from CPTSD. I would say my journey has evolved from often desiring suicide to loving myself, life and the World. I would say I have recovered and now my journey is about self development, but I can't say when the tipping point came.

I've been playing the saxophone for thirty years. For the first year I wondered if it were ever possible to play without feeling I would loose consciousness: all that huffing and puffing. I observed one day I didn't feel like that anymore, but can't detect even a definitive period when the giddiness left me. Blowing didn't require effort; I had 'tipped over' without realizing. If you're in trouble right now, if you're struggling, please know this: I've been there. This book will help. One day you'll just blow through life. It will happen.

I have read a few books on Childhood Sexual Abuse (CSA) and trauma recovery: each played an important role in my journey, but those written by therapists, in my opinion, are possibly hamstrung by the 'Omerta'/code of the profession. They can't tell you what to do. Largely, they present evidence leaving you to discern what is applicable and any practical support gets drowned out with the obligatory validation of research accompanied by vague, sometimes contrary, interpretation. Also, they may use flowery language (psychobabble – there's a lot out there) ultimately offering an explanation of where you are at and why, but not how to move forward.

Know this: You have survived this far, you are therefore equipped with the strength and resource to recover.

And also, know this from the outset: your soul is born pure and remains pure. I now believe, an understanding gained from recovery, our spirits always rise to the light. I've learnt to let it.

'Letting it' takes a lot of hard work. It's the longest, hardest task I have undertaken, colossal but doable. An

'Odyssey' is the description used by a great man who has saved many survivors of CSA.

The evil (there's no way else to label it) of childhood abuse stains the soul, but does not irreparably damage. You can clean and fix it. The evil affects your behavior patterns, your thoughts and your feelings, but you can change these....if you CHOOSE to.

Again, let's be very clear, no one else is going to do it for you.

It's most likely you are reading this because you are a survivor, but know this.....and this is essential for recovery....you need to accept this....

Your recovery is your responsibility.
(pack your own parachute)

I urge you to grasp the above otherwise you are susceptible to becoming stuck. Playing the role of victim can feel safe. It's easy to do, going around and around in the same circle moaning that the World is wrong: blaming and off loading (can be abusive). But no one is going to directly take the pain away, no therapist, or anyone, or any one thing will do it for you or should claim to be able to.

Perhaps being stuck in the same patterns of feelings, behavior and thoughts, implies not having truly accepted the trauma?

If you are a survivor of abuse and therefore trauma, it was inflicted on you. This is unfair. The word 'unfair' is a massive understatement, I get that. The control of you, your boundaries, your body, your life spirit, was taken away. You were violated. You were abused. You are now charged with the responsibility of repairing the damage which creates enormous resent. But I view it like this: I am taking back control of my life by recovering. I am not relying on anyone else to take control of my recovery, therefore I control me. This is **empowerment.**

Getting over the resent is seemingly impossible. It haunted me, but I found it just left me (like the 'huffing & puffing'). Know that it will. But to expect, or hope, a person or an organization will take away the pain of trauma will get you stuck which retards recovery allowing effects of trauma to continue and tip over into self perpetuating victim hood.

If you were abused as a child: you were traumatized, perhaps repeatedly. As a child you were easy to manipulate. IT WAS NOT YOUR FAULT. How you physically and emotionally reacted was perfectly natural. To go on and survive the complexities of life with the burden of trauma is a gigantic achievement, no matter the extent of the abuse. You should be very proud of yourself.

Now you are going to recover. The first step is to make the decision you are going to recover. 'I will recover' will be your 'go to' mantra on this Odyssey you are on, or are about to undertake. Once you have made the decision the journey is easier, especially at four a.m. when alone and the suicide snake wraps around you.

Your mission is to recover; to become the full you waiting inside and, if you choose, help other thrivers and join the growing throng combating abuse.

I believe it is our responsibility to do the above. Why? Because we need to stop what happened to us from happening to children and people. We have a duty as a species to evolve for the better. We have a duty to become authentic adults as individuals and as a collective. A cornerstone is to face into and deal with abuse.

BTW - let's establish an important fact here before we carry on – know that childhood abuse/trauma survivors largely become 'protectors' often found in the caring professions, keen to help and protect others and/or in roles as guardians, eager to prevent what happened to them happening to others……

3. Trauma

I couldn't find a satisfactory definition that didn't need some elaboration, so I'm not going to write one.

Trauma affects the body, mind and emotions. Trauma affects our perception of ourselves and the World. Trauma affects our neural avenues. Trauma gets retained in the body and affects the way we do and don't feel. Trauma affects our spiritual connection with life.

Signs of Trauma –

Problems sleeping & concentrating. Feeling separated from the World. Depression. Often anxious. Attitude of self pity. Lying/manipulative. Forgetful. Self Doubt. Hyper judgmental/critical of others and yourself. Addictive behavour in all/any of its guises - bingeing. Consumed by shame. Catastrophising – people say you exaggerate. Often panicking. Often late/rushing in a state of angst. Emotional numbness. Emotional (inappropriate) outbursts/explosions. Feelings of despair, listless, hopelessness. Worrying – imagining negative outcomes. Craving withdrawal from environment. Distrust of others. Fragile boundaries. Hyper sensitive to (perceived) boundary infringement. Paranoia. Needing/allowing/submitting others to manage practical aspects of your life. Constant need to control your environment. Chaotic. Limited awareness of consequences of behavour. Relationship problems – stuck in/evoking destructive patterns. Multiple partners. Limited emotional range. Quick to anger/seek conflict. Inflexible – opinionated/willful. Often frustrated. Black or white thinking. Irritable. Blaming. Arrogance. Grandiosity.

Superiority. Attention seeking. Unforgiving – won't let go. Need to win. Obsessive behavour. Fear of expressing anger. Fear of being exposed as a fraud - imposter syndrome. Pretending to be helpless. Fear of intimacy. Flashbacks. Feeling the World is 'echoed' /empty. Self abuse. Self hatred. Sexual dysfunction. Feeling of unworthiness. Feeling lesser than others. Unable to accept nurturing. Inabilty to accept compliments. Feeling isolated/detached from the World. Wanting to be isolated. Feelings of deserving of abuse. Feeling inadequate. Self image as a failure. Feeling violent. Inability to express vulnerability. Need to perfect – must be competent. Fears. Reckless risk taking. Paralysing fear of any risks. Compartmentalising people/life/experiences. Inability to say 'no'. Inability to protect boundaries. Suspicious of others – perceived ulterior motives. Feeling trapped. 'Flapping' / seemingly busy but achieving little. Feeling responsible for everything. Refusing to be accountable for behavior. Suicide ideation…

Wishing you were someone else…someone 'normal' like all the others.

Hmmm……

How have you reacted to the list?

There isn't a person on Earth that doesn't experience some of these at some point in their lives.

Given you are reading this book it's likely you recognize several of these in yourself, or deal with people displaying these characteristics. On recognition, it is worth registering the thoughts and feelings created; noting the sensation of reading something that moves a thought from 'the tip of your tongue' fully into your conscious mind.

The realization, 'whooa…that's me,' or 'I get it – that's why they are like that', can stop you in your tracks.

The feeling of identification: 'yes, that's me', seeing what you know, or suspected, about yourself in black and white combats confusion and doubt, thereby assisting your recovery i.e. if you know what you are dealing with you can tackle it. Or, if close to an abuse survivor you can begin to look past the behavior to the cause and therefore accept, understand, and even help.

There is good news –

Your conscious recognition starts the process of being able to put space between you and the 'issue/s' allowing you to make choices: 'Oh yeah, that's me…' (conscious recognition) verses unconsciously continuing the same pattern. In other words, the conscious recognition sets up the first stage of change.

I didn't invent these symptoms (although I have endured plenty). Better qualified people than me identified them; therefore you are on well trodden ground. There is plenty of knowledge, help and wisdom to be gathered. **Plus, you are far, far, far from being alone.** The list of traits tells you it is possible to do something about them. It is. That's why they've been gathered up and written down. They are not 'oh dear bad luck,' rather, 'here they are, acknowledge them, move forward and do something about them [if you choose]'

Please accept that there is no hierarchy when it comes to trauma. This is an accepted precept. I have met many survivors, notably of childhood trauma (physical, emotional, neglect, sexual) of varying degrees, and others that have endured trauma in adulthood and there is a commonality in the effects.

NB. You don't have to have endured trauma in your childhood, or otherwise, to experience any of the above conditions.

Part B - Tools

Following are a list of tools and techniques plus my views on them; my views as I write (therefore they are not necessarily right or suitable for you).

Recovering from mental illness, trauma and the effects of abuse is imprecise. Your journey will sometimes appear to zig zag and then go in circles. Some tools/knowledge will have no use then it will, then it won't. You'll hold some views and later change them. The journey of recovery is best done with flexibility in its heart.

Below is a list of things you can do to help you – not in order of priority (except for No.1) – no doubt you will find others.

1. Self Care (& self compassion).
2. Mindset.
3. Reading about Mental health issues /Trauma and CA.
4. Therapy.
5. Group work - sharing.
5. Support Network.
6. Body Work.
7. Reaching out & Declaration.
8. 'You Stuff' (expression & creativity)…play

1. Self Care (& self compassion)

Despite my earlier disclaimer I will stand my ground and be absolute on this one: ***The – most – important – thing – in – recovery – is – SELF CARE!***

Take the oxygen first – Like on the plane – Always - Every time - All the time - Your well being first - Before anyone else's.

For many periods you may not accept that your life is a gift. It is. You are responsible for you, your life. You are responsible for you more than anyone else is responsible for you. You are more responsible for you than you are for any(adult)body else.

And...every other adult is primarily responsible for themselves.

Recovery is founded in self care. Self care forms the fundamental root of recovery.

You have a responsibility to live the best way for you.

It may well be the trauma/s you experienced were inflicted on you therefore, even momentarily, you had no control over your being, but now you have & it will stay this way if you choose it to be so!

Mantra : 'It [cause of trauma] was not my fault'

Keep going back to this one. Go round and round with it. Even if it just sits on the surface, just keep going back to it…

Self care is one thing in your life you can control. You need to allow self care. It can be hard to let go of feeling shameful, unworthy, and therefore allow yourself to look after you. A lack of self worth may be so ingrained you don't recognize you endure it. You may treat yourself without the care you ought to and this is the normal for you. Even if brought to your attention, you may still feel you are below deserving self care.

I am about to rave on about self care methods. I am currently drug and drink free, up in the mornings in all weather, stretching, jogging and (here's the weird bit) having a cold shower (I never thought I'd ever actually look forward to a cold shower, but I strongly recommend it – invigorating & I find it cleanses me of morning anxiety), so in all, I'm feeling very righteous. All very new behavior, so please understand this cross I'm dragging is a novel experience and appended with a fair bit of preaching. But, trust me, I've been at the other end of the seesaw: getting out of bed smoking a joint first thing and chain smoking another (numbing out) in order to cope with spending the day being me, it's going to be too hard otherwise. Just as you began your journey of recovery it is also baby steps with the self care, and as you go you will keep adding to the routine and replacing bad things with good.

One thing that disappears when people lose interest for life is care in their appearance. So let's make the decision to reverse this. Start a daily routine beginning with taking pride in your self image which initiates the habit of caring for your self physically, all of which builds self worth and, in turn, resilience. Please forgive the condescension but I have been there, unable to look at myself in the mirror because of the self loathing, but having made the decision to recover I figured I've got to start somewhere and that somewhere was taking care of me. Self respect grows when fostered and people in turn treat you with respect, becoming a reinforcing circular thing. I made the effort everyday even if I knew I wouldn't be going out the door. And how about a tidy up and clean of your cave? Put on the radio, a cheery station – get connected. Send out some messages, say hello without expecting anything back.

I recall for a good few months when seriously struggling mindfully doing the above and since heard this is the way forward. You don't need to ask much of yourself, and never mind the World it can take care of itself. Adopt a simple routine everyday and you will begin to feel better about you. And do everything mindfully; I recall during the early part of my breakdown narrating progress whilst vacuum cleaning, given that was all I was able to do which is okay, and continually applying positive self talk about what a great job I was doing. A straight forward routine every day provides manageable activities to engage in, and you will know in advance what you are going to do. You won't be consumed with angst worrying if you should be doing something or destructively staring into the abyss, because now you have a plan. You will find yourself just doing it, doing things for you, helping yourself. Get yourself a track to go down. A track is a planned daily routine loaded with self care stuff done mindfully. We are all simple creatures at heart, we all like routine and investing in a nice routine of stuff is all you need to ask of yourself. Do that and you are doing just fine.

Enacting self care fuels an increase in self worth. Self care is on-going nourishment recovery feeds on, and increasing self worth is a vital building block for recovery.

I was informed one of the biggest concepts people struggle to cope with is uncertainty. We wall ourselves up against uncertainty *(was it Seneca who claimed we wall ourselves up against death/the unknown – often with possessions we don't need: we can look back at the junk and feel justified – or hope that we will)*. We know what we like and we like what we know. We like habit and predictability. Being traumatized, for one, enhances the sense that life is uncertain. Many go on after trauma in crippling fear of life, even if the fear is buried and never truly acknowledged. But on our journey one thing we can control is, self care. We can choose to administer it to ourselves.

Two personal anecdotes:

My birthday was coming up a few years ago and I was someway into my recovery, still raw. I decided I wanted a leather jacket. I must have my clothes fit and feel just so, possibly brandable as autistic, or 'on the spectrum' as my wife puts it, and perhaps also due to a traumatized childhood – I have read stuff about this being a symptom i.e. the chronic need to have things we touch and wear 'just so'. I wanted a leather jacket exactly waist length (top of my trousers), zip straight down the middle, no labels, absolutely plain, not patch pockets but with zips, no pleats, no elasticized bits, no collar, simple round neck, super soft light tan leather, and an inside zip pocket....I looked obsessively all over London. I gave up. We went on holiday to Ibiza. I found one in a shop in a town we were visiting for the day. It was perfect and reasonably priced but I hadn't got enough money with me. Good, I had an excuse not to buy. It was 'okay' they said, 'they would save it'. I told them I may not be back: another excuse. It took an enormous amount of energy and conflicting self talk to allow myself to go back a few days later. They had sold the jacket. I was relieved, I didn't have to buy it; I had been denied which I was comfortable with because I wasn't allowed, because I wasn't worthy. 'But the other shop might have one, just wait' they said. I panicked. Another appeared. It was perfect in every way. I took my credit card this time but couldn't remember my pin number exactly. I was saved, it was going to be okay, I was going to be disappointed, a feeling I was familiar and comfortable with, I am allowed disappointment. But on the third attempt of entering numbers the transaction, to my surprise, went through. They wrapped it up and I walked outside on this stunningly beautiful day, sat on a concrete traffic bollard and crumbled and sobbed: I was allowed this jacket. The realization of my lack of self worth had surfaced during my journey of recovery. By observing my reactions to the process of buying the jacket I could acknowledge them. I experienced the intense sadness of having carried this lack of self worth buried inside all my life. But the jacket also symbolized a turning point. I am worthy [another significant mantra].

Further on, I spent about four months recognizing that 'hey....this is what having recovered feels like; this is what it is...' and feeling at peace with life, finally. Then my wife entered the flat after she'd initially popped to the optician with a minor vision issue where she was advised to go immediately to hospital. She'd sent a text between the two places I didn't understand about being delayed. After arriving home and closing the front door she announced, 'I've been diagnosed with a brain tumour'. I'm not sure, after two operations and intensive radiotherapy, we truly accept she has one (it's still there and growing – again, as I write - apparently). The short of the long and deep in terms of emotions and mental processes we went through, was to find stuff we could do about it. Having recovered from a monumental nervous breakdown caused by CSA, I had a map. Self care first. We stepped up the get fit and healthy thing big time. This, we figured, is something we can do to positively combat what is happening to us. Something out of our control has happened but we can **control how we react to it**. *As such, we can directly do something about improving our health.*

It is not what happens to you, but how you react to it that matters ~ Epictetus [Stoic Philosopher]

Incidentally, if you are a survivor of childhood abuse/trauma and wonder if recovery is possible and if so what it is like and concerned you will be forever flawed and weakened in some way, let me tell you this: I know people have always viewed me as a strong person because that is the persona I projected, but the tumor news would have scared me so much previously I would have feared coping and needed a crutch in the form of drink and drugs. Having recovered from CSA it didn't occur to me I wouldn't cope. I haven't had to even consciously stay away from the drugs and drink – they just don't call to me at all anymore. Plus, I knew without a second thought, or even a first, I'd be strong enough i.e. able to experience and be with and process any sense of hopelessness, fear, vulnerability etc, whilst maintaining faith. I knew instinctively I'd strong enough for the both of us.

I'd already been to the very bottom of the deep dark well and come back up. I was holding the small round coins (read The Well of Grief by David Whyte). So can you. And know this: I sit on the loo just like you (one of grandma's – bless her, raised six children on her own pre the welfare state – favourite sayings when explaining how not to be fearful of someone)! I'm a human.... Also, as an aside, it is important to recognize that if you endured familial abuse there will very likely have been others close by in your childhood that fulfilled positive supportive roles (like my wonderful Grandmas – both).

I won't drone on about diet. I personally get preachy if I'm doing 'the right thing'. We all know something about eating right, although 'they' do chop and change their minds quite a lot. I will say one thing though: my wife went for a second brain operation, a duplicate of the first, the difference being second time round after another six and half hours of surgery she was greeted by me with a homemade smoothie loaded with goodness, and one twice a day thereafter i.e. each hospital visit. Her everything (blood pressure, vitamins, iron, cognitive skills even, etc…wotnot, blah,) were measured as part of the procedure after some days and all were way better than after the first op'. This smoothie programme continued at home and I noticed a marked difference in her recovery. I had recalled a TV series on autopsies (hmm…not my choice) one featuring the man that was Patrick Swayze and how he defied cancer for so long via smoothies according to the doctor interviewed.

Exercise! Need to say more? There is endless material out there explaining why it's a good idea, but the positive effects on one's mental health cannot be underestimated. Trick is to keep it regular, like every day. I'm not talking about an intimidating athletic campaign you are likely to find ways to avoid, simple everyday exercise; getting out in the light and walking, vigorously if possible. Exercise will simply flush negativity out of you. You don't need equipment. You don't need excuses either. It ***is*** about you, remember? Exercise is fundamental. One of the cornerstones of the recovery building has got one word on it, 'exercise'.

Can't sleep? Get out of bed at the same time every day regardless, + exercise in the light.

Nailing down the basics is the key to recovery; self care, diet, exercise and other stuff like 'you' time.

'Doh, Ray, Me....' as the beautiful Ms Andrews taught us – by repeating the basics we are better equipped to improvise our way through life as it demands.

'You time' is time for you. What do you like to do (that isn't unhealthy)...nothing at all?....doing nothing at all is a good one.

I've always been so riddled with angst that doing nothing could be a torture. I had to be 'achieving' something in a manic angst riddled fashion – running from my own feelings. Now I find I've a natural talent for doing naff all without any conscience whatsoever!

Listening to music, cooking….doing stuff you like to do. Allow yourself. Allow yourself regularly. Never forget what you like to do. Have a list at hand for when you feel like you are dropping down again (you may well – its okay, it happens). The stuff you like to do are always there waiting for you, in your survival kitbag. Those things will form an oasis you can head for. Once you have allocated and sanctioned time to the activity when indulging you're less inclined to have the monkey in the mind drag you into negative thinking, rather: 'all my worries can go on hold for two hours whilst I do this'.

Along with looking after yourself physically there is self soothing which is a critical tool for your journey. This is the nurturing of you, your spiritual self. This is doing, or not doing, stuff to put you in a safe place and help you be calm. And it doesn't involve destructive behavior like drugs or drink or gambling.

For those of us, especially, neglected in childhood with no soothing by care givers to support us through difficult times (*we have spent a lifetime relying on only ourselves to compensate us for any hardships, and struggle to trust others to give us care*), be ready with self soothing activities to aid your journey; if predefined, when in distress you won't flap about panicking wondering what to do with yourself which won't help, it could make things worse. And keep the self soothing activities, or non activities, in your daily routine.

On a similar note: what about chilling? Years ago I shared a house with a chap who served as a soldier in Northern Ireland. It had affected him deeply: he was traumatised. On return from every street patrol, dodging from house to house in genuine fear of snipers whilst facing constant abuse from the locals, they loosened their clothes, lay on beds set wide apart and, by order, did not move or make a sound i.e. forced relaxation. Make time to relax every day in a way that feels right. Look into things like meditation. There are various methods but they are fundamentally about breathing. Relaxing is about conscious breathing; in essence, breathing deeply and slowly.

The way you breathe directly affects your thinking and feeling.

For example: an inhale shorter in time than the exhale stimulates your parasympathetic nervous system which sends the message to self you are not under attack and therefore safe (I understand this is the pattern we adopt when asleep = relaxed). Worth popping that technique into the kitbag for when panic starts to get a grip.

Conversely, panting, which happens when we are stressed, is a way of pumping the body with oxygen to prepare for fight or flight in turn triggering release of adrenaline. If your breathing is shallow and fast it signals to the nervous system you are in danger, so either flight, fight, freeze. All the logic you have, everything you have listened to or read, all the wisdom you possess evaporates leaving panic but there is one thing can stop it, conscious control of your breathe. It is a powerful thing.

Separating time out everyday to take deep long slow breaths - got to be a good thing.

There is another massive thing you can do for yourself to help you heal…..employ ***self compassion*** – make it your balm, a primary tool.

I know that beyond physical abuse there are other insidious and no less damaging ways a child is abused, such as neglect which directly affects the child's sense of self worth, in turn disabling self compassion. Being traumatized in adulthood will be the same. There is the strong propensity to feel as though you are always and only a victim and nothing else, that you are not worthy of self compassion. Wrong. 'Stinking thinking'.

A lot of recovery is about recognizing the behaviors not serving you anymore and recognizing that your self image is possibly wrong too.

So where do I get self compassion? This self love? This self acceptance?

One way is to accept it is already there: you don't have to bring it in. You are reading this for you because you care about you. Self compassion is evoked by repeated practice. Self compassion feeds on practice and mantras that reinforce it. Don't hope, wait, prompt, or need compassion from others thereby inviting disappointment and despair if your expectancy isn't met which serves to be disempowering, i.e. depending on reinforcement from others serves to relinquish control of you. And self compassion is especially helpful if applied when addressing a pattern of behavior you are looking to negate. Apply understanding and forgiveness of yourself when facing into a toxic pattern of thought and behavior you are aiming to disarm. Apply understanding and forgiveness rather than berating yourself; you'll find it actually makes the transition to a new pattern easier. The self compassion is lubricant aiding movement from one negative pattern to its positive replacement [more].

As you go on your journey on a cerebral level i.e. gaining understanding of how the trauma came about, how it affected you and therefore the way you engage with the World, keep applying self compassion. Apply self compassion when viewing your thought patterns and behaviors developed to help you cope and survive. Apply self compassion when you *feel* you are 'failing' in your recovery (chances are at times you will feel you are), rather than berating yourself. If you choose self compassion you will heal more easily. Its okay, you are allowed. Give yourself permission.

Twenty seven adult male survivors of childhood sexual abuse met for a weekend. I wasn't sure about it before I went.

'I don't need this, bunch of blokes moaning, feeling sorry for themselves, droning on about feelings, doing silly group tasks...I'm done with this recovery business, way through the worst, this may drag me backwards...' was the tone of my chattering monkey.
First meeting in a circle at the introduction session I sobbed, ignited by the thought of all these men having been through what I had suffered, their courage to join in with this group and the sheer force of truth by our being together open and vulnerable. But there was a twang of shame at having 'let' this experience, this gathering in a circle, immediately 'get through to me'. I told my other survivor friend (he didn't attend) how I felt about this after the weekend by way of expressing and extinguishing the shame, and by way of conveying the intensity of the occasion, to which he responded...

'Greg, you gave them permission.'
I had made it okay to express their feelings by expressing mine.
Nourish your roots. Nourish the soul.

2. Mindset

Five important points –

1. Flexibility
2. Expectancy
3. Acceptance
4. Self honesty and responsibility
5. Decide

1. Flexibility: To recover is about change. To recover you have to change. Change the way you react to life. Change your beliefs, your logic, how you project yourself, how you view yourself; change your habits, physiology, etc, etc…..this is about deconstructing yourself and then putting yourself back together…in my opinion. And change in one aspect of you will affect another. Recovery is about moving and keeping moving. That is what change is: movement. The big problem/blockage to change you will face is – fear of change [more]. The thing blocking you from recovering is….you…you need to get out of your own way. There is only one person stopping you from being flexible, you. Don't blame anyone or anything else – not anymore.

2. Expectancy: I met a 5'3'' half French half Italian chap called Aldo many moons ago when I was drifting around Asia. He told me how he used to be into motorbike sidecar racing. He was the chap that hung onto the sidecar. I've seen on board film footage of this activity since and simply watching

on TV made my heart race, doing about 160mph around the Isle of Mann in an awkward position clinging to the sidecar with, at times, their nose just 4'' from the ground. Knowing Aldo this was an ideal activity for him. He told how it wasn't unusual for the vehicle to go out of control and crash. He told me he would *expect* this to happen. With expectancy he didn't freeze and panic. He was able to think ahead and do stuff to lessen the potential damage to himself. He described how, by way of giving an example, he was flying through the air fully off the ground towards a tree and rather than think 'oh no it looks like I'm going to hit a tree' and freeze (wham). Instead he pointed the soles of his feet at the tree, bent his legs and twisted his body so on collision he bounced around the side of it. The impact wasn't pleasant but not as bad as it could have been. If you have some expectancy then you can deal with stuff. Having expectancy helps you accept stuff. Once you have accepted something you can deal with it. If something comes up on your journey, having expectancy helps: the surprise is weakened.

3. Acceptance: This is very hard. There is stuff about my childhood I am still struggling to accept. An adult being so cruel to a child. What was it that enabled them to keep repeating the cruelty? I understand the situation I was in as a small boy, to an extent, because I have read about the construct of a dysfunctional family where abuse is occurring, but truly accepting it…? Similarly, before I could conquer being an addict I had to accept I was an addict. If you recognize behavioral traits in the lists given earlier then doing something about it/them requires acceptance; you are this way, and

make the decision to change. Also, accept the change is your liability.

As I write my wife is resting on this rainy, grim late Thursday afternoon. This morning we went to the hospital to meet with a radiotherapy doctor and brain surgeon to be told that despite the intense radiotherapy on the bit of the tumor they couldn't cut out of her brain, even during the second operation, it has grown. Our options are now limited in number and potential effect. She wants an answer to everything going forward. Firstly, we needed to understand and ***accept*** *the situation we're in before we made any decisions.*

Before the first operation they said the tumour wasn't malignant, they would cut it out and everything would be fine. After the operation and a period of recovery [easy to say in a sentence] we went back expecting them to confirm everything was okay. They didn't and we were shocked. I felt very angry which I managed to suppress or more importantly, not express impulsively. My wife was dazed. They'd left some of the tumor in but it should be okay, it shouldn't grow and if it does it will take years. We went back after a scan some months later expecting them to confirm all was stable but they told us the tumor had grown already and they needed to operate again and then give radiotherapy, but that should do it. So we went ahead with both. She had a scan recently and we went back in this morning. This time we were hoping for the best but were prepared, to an extent (feet towards the tree), for the worst i.e. we had some expectancy; we had some expectancy to be surprised (ambushed). As a result we were able to ask questions and comprehend information when they told us that the radiotherapy hadn't worked and the remaining part of the tumor had grown.

Expect that your recovery feels like it is zig zagging sometimes, going forwards and next 'seemingly', going backwards. I now don't view it like this: we are wrong to think we have gone backwards, we haven't: we needed to re-expose ourselves to an area of recovery to fully learn the lesson.

Expect the really hard yards to take longer than you first imagine. Expect your recovery to be harder and more demanding than you want it to be, most probably much harder. Expect that it will be more complex than you think. Accept all of the above. Once you accept, the journey will be easier.

That's nice Greg thank you for that.

Hey, feet up!

And….expect that you will do it.
(Because you've already made the decision – right?).

There's a Roman saying, I believe, which goes something like, 'you are strapped to the cart of life, you can get dragged along complaining, or you can choose to walk along side whistling.' You are on this journey, you may as well commit to it. And when you do it becomes easier.

4. In my opinion your main ally in recovery is brutal self honesty, and few of us are capable of this……
You need to keep pushing your nose back to self honesty. Plus, your self awareness needs to expand and with *work* i.e. self honesty, it will. This is an important part of recovery: an important part of the need to keep moving, to keep evolving, to keep changing. Self honesty ignites the fuse of movement;

it gets you out of blockages, negative patterns, denial, and therefore getting stuck. But self honesty takes work. It can hurt. It can hurt accepting truths about oneself, your life.
Self honesty is an ingredient of the space required to recognize and put between you and it. The 'you' is that conscious 'you' that observes, and the 'it' is the destructive behavior, thought and/or feeling [more].

A brutal truth you have to grasp and accept: if you were abused as a child, or have suffered trauma - it does not come with compensation.

'I was abused/traumatized so I am entitled to live as I feel fit without regard for others. I am entitled to behave in a destructive way. I am entitled to perpetually moan and feel sorry for myself and therefore, in effect, be abusive to those in my sphere'. Having been abused/traumatised is a *reason* for destructive behavior, but it is not an *excuse.*

Recovery, however, does come with compensation, in a big way.

Yes, we have along way to go as a species in terms of evolving into creating truly responsible nurturing societies. But leaning back and *expecting* the current society to take responsibility for your issues will not work. You have to make the first move and keep driving along your own recovery. The people that recover from operations most quickly are those that push themselves to get moving. Laying around pressing the buzzer for the nurse does not lead to recovery. Yes, there is help out there which may feel woeful at times, but there is an old phrase, '...help comes to those that help themselves...' recovery from trauma is no exception. And remember, with the decision made to recover, having made the choice to do something about it, you are empowered.

It's you that needs to change. It will be hard, but much easier than trying to change the rest of the World to fit around you. Accept you may have to change nearly everything you believe, change a multitude of behavior patterns, feelings and thoughts. People don't like change. People are good at criticizing and seeing what is wrong with things and others, but not themselves. This, however, is balanced against destructive self criticism. I am saying the line between brutal self honesty and destructive self criticism can get fuzzy. As a trauma survivor you may well be an expert at destructive self criticism to the point of self hatred (I know this one well). It is a paradox: the balance between self honesty and destructive self criticism. For example: 'why do I feel the need to create a drama so as to attract attention so often?' vs 'oh, I am such a vacuous needy loser?' The former begins with self honesty and leads to more self awareness and change. The latter is just plain destructive.

Paradox: combines contradictory features.

Drawing the line of separation in a paradox is a challenge with many issues in recovery, not just self honesty verses criticism, and I find it shifts as I go. And the process of defining the line can become complex if you allow it. You can get analysis paralysis repeatedly dissecting an issue attempting to separate contradictions. But I believe that simplicity is where recovery is unleashed, rather than purely via understanding complex psychotherapy.

5 Make the decision (we've covered this). Even if the decision feels like you've made it at a superficial level. It doesn't matter. Just make it. Then it's done. It's

made. No need to re-visit it. Keep it simple. 'I will recover'. The end.

Once the decision has been made all else will fall in line; information and people will come to you to help you on your journey. Expect that you will challenge the decision so no surprise when you do, but the decision has been made, so that's that.

Imagine laying foundation stones to build on, shifting focus from one to another dependent on what suits at any one time, and only you will know which instinctively you will: you'll know what is right and wrong for you at any given moment. The objective is to keep moving, avoid getting stuck by succumbing, for example, to the presence of 'triggers' i.e. allowing them to dictate your life by constantly avoiding them and therefore causing yourself to be defined by the trauma [more]. In essence, keep a discerning mind on different techniques and give them a try. I think this applies to life in general: being open, but discerning, to new things, thoughts and beliefs. In essence, recovery is about staying flexible.

It's not necessarily the strongest, the fittest or the most intelligent that survive – it's the adaptable (flexible).

3. Reading about Mental health issues /Trauma and CA

I'm not going to recommend any reading. I've read several self help/recovery/philosophical/therapy books either several times, half read and ditched, skim read once, others several times with intensity, remembered some, forgotten others, others I'm a disciple of and bang on about but nobody agrees, and some people will say a certain book is great and I think its rubbish. It's subjective.

Knowledge does not release you. Just having information is not enough.

As part of recovery I went back to painting. My inner child [more] did it – little Gregory. I went to night school and figured I'd still got it and upgraded. I got a web site and got involved with a charity that occupied unused buildings in London and let offices to artists to paint in. At the end of each period we would have our own show, invite friends etc, put on some music have a few nibbles and a giggle. We'd display our work, people would mingle around and I would sidle up to anyone lurking near my dozen or so paintings.

'Which one do you prefer?' was my opening question (rather than 'what do you think?' the response to which might upset one of my many sensitivities).

If I'd drawn a bar chart the next day with painting titles on the X axis (bottom one) and number of people on the Y axis (side one), the bars would have been about equal in height. The same number of people liked a painting I thought was rubbish as did the painting I thought was good.

Moral: there is no accounting for taste (without the cynicism). Possibly, everyone thinks their taste is the best. It took me some time to grasp the result of this 'painting test', but how could they be wrong? It wasn't as if there were two (in my mind) good pictures and people couldn't choose between them. No. The number of people liking each painting was equal, and I hasten to add that some of them, in my opinion, are terrible.

Quick side story on this note: I saw an art competition advertised with a healthy reward; the submissions were to be titled 'Progress'. I noticed my wife going to work carrying a plastic container from a supermarket shelf as part of a 'meal deal' with slices of apples in and I had an 'aaha' moment. So I painted a big container with 'Big Exploitation Company plc' on the lid, a factory chopping and processing and billowing smoke, machines with exhausts pumping out toxic fumes picking the perfect fruit from trees, and children looking at the discarded plastic tubs floating in the sea. Not a bad idea (irony!?) except the execution was awful. In our street anything of value left on the pavement would be adopted. The flat was filling with paintings so I put this one outside (too embarrassed to enter it in the competition). It went. Sometime later I visited a mate in his office and it was hanging on the wall! He was very defensive when I suggested it was rubbish and animated whilst telling me why it was a good painting, plus he couldn't understand why anyone would put it out on the street! After listening to his viewpoint, which I hadn't considered, I informed him it was upside down (I kid you not – I mean, how did he manage that? It actually had writing on it, and trees! It was simply that bad!). And I told him why I knew and the story behind the creative process. Given this insightful information (highlighting the existence of the trees took some doing) coupled with the offer of adding my signature (in any corner of his choosing I made clear), I asked him for two hundred quid; his brusque response implied he didn't consider this proposal to be of any interest and subsequently wouldn't be giving me any money.

The take away? I have my journey & you have yours + we can see things differently + there is definitely no accounting for taste!

In terms of recovery, especially when it comes to reading, what suits you may not suit another. One book that springs to mind is worshipped among the therapy cognoscenti and survivors which I and my wife (who reads a lot and I think she has a talent for picking a well written book) think is drivel. You might think the same about this one.

If you are in anyway a 'reader' (guess you must be) then this book perhaps ought not to be your only book. Reading about trauma is a cerebral activity enabling understanding of your situation. Understanding your situation helps you to accept it. Acceptance leads to recovery. But being discerning is vital. Just one book with one way of viewing the way forward may be all you need. However, you may find an issue raised doesn't agree with you causing you to feel the 'one' book is right and you are wrong, therefore you may begin to question yourself in a negative way.

'If the book says it is so then it must be and there must be something wrong with me.'

A bit like religion i.e. 'you must do and think like this' (…really?). Not so with recovery. This is about you and what you feel comfortable with. No one can impose a right way for you.

Some years ago, not that long in terms of humankind's presence on this planet, the 'experts' were drilling holes in people's heads by way of 'curing' them. That was 'right' then. Similarly, what is considered 'right' now in terms of treatment may we reflect on in the future with contempt? (Profuse use of psychotropic drugs I suspect).

My uncle was subjected to numerous electric shock treatments (ECT electroconvulsive therapy). My wife witnessed it when starting out as a nurse. She said it was barbaric and very disturbing, recalling the memory upsets her. And in a recent documentary about a female serial killer an expert referred to her mother having had ECT just before giving birth which would have 'almost certainly' affected the development of the baby's prefrontal cortex (controls social behavior), added to which, the killer was also sexually abused by her father. 1. ECT good or bad? 2. Nature or nurture? (The latter for both, I think).

A considerable portion of stuff by Freud, once the hailed messiah of psychotherapy, is now discounted. Again, what theories and 'accepted' beliefs will we look back on in the future with disdain?

I understand it was Freud who believed that anyone over thirty was beyond help! He was perhaps hindered being unaware of neuroplasticity.

We learn and move on.

Take in ideas through your own filter. Material you feel is irrelevant may cause you to feel no one really knows what they are doing when it comes to understanding and decoding your issues, that no one really knows the answers. This can be scary. I felt this way at first when I was desperate for information. Prior to my breakdown I'd read the odd book by psychologists/therapists out of interest i.e. eating for the sake of eating rather than hunger. Later in my desperate state the first book I read about surviving childhood sexual trauma was recommended by a support group. I loaded so much hope into it but thought it superficial which added to a sense of hopelessness i.e. when I looked for information I found it to be thin, 'oh no, the lifejacket is too small'. Fortunately with the next book I struck gold, read it six times and it proved to be a magical stepping stone leading to the weekend mentioned, and subsequent belonging to a group of survivors. So don't be alarmed if you don't immediately find the answers written in print, if this one doesn't fit for example, try another. I've read a few and eerrrrr…….well…. 'keep the positives and leave the rest behind.'

Conversely, I am just now part of a group of survivors wherein a brother raved about a book, the others expressed an interest and another had also read it. After a discussion several decided this was the book for them. I read the sample on-line and did a modicum of investigation. It was about, given a view from not having actually read it (so you can discount the following), splitting oneself down into various previous ages. It advocated the separating out of oneself into younger selves by way of enabling you to communicate with, listen to, and understand the 'you's' in you.

If you were traumatized as a child then rescuing your inner child (or you at a younger age e.g. the age when the abuse occurred) is relevant. I am far from alone in the belief that healing from childhood trauma is critically about giving your inner child a voice and allowing the child within you to come out and be heard. To share her or his pain and be listened to, acknowledged and believed. To be ultimately and vitally, loved, respected and made to feel safe as your inner child within you deserves. But for me just now I am not into the idea of fragmenting myself further and potentially making my journey anymore complicated, I am consciously simplifying so this practice doesn't fit my journey. I am not especially criticizing this approach, although I am skeptical. My reasoning is I think it has the potential to give effects of the trauma more fuel rather than take them away: after healing each fragmented part of you, then what? Go on to maintain these fragments/personas?! I think recovery is about heading towards a sense of wholeness. To me this practice has the potential, if not navigated consciously, to perpetuate a fragmented self. Compartmentalizing life is a trait of survivors (one of mine); it is a control and therefore safety mechanism whereby the survivor separates things/people/situations/experiences into distinct 'boxes/categories', and I suspected this 'selves' approach might accentuate this. I am suggesting that despite a lack of knowledge of this philosophy I sensed it is not right for me. Similarly, you will read or hear about approaches that don't suit you. Remember, your journey is your journey and it is exactly right at any given moment. You will be like an animal, a cat perhaps, that only has to sniff something even just once to know it is not for you.

'Perhaps I simply pop it into my kitbag and maybe take a view on it later, given it serves me better to keep a discerning and flexible outlook on concepts rather than dismiss them outright forever. Hey, if it works for others then why not. Maybe I'll take a look again later. In summary, I am not obliged to make a philosophy fit'.

Another concept raised recently was Epigenetics in relation to trauma. After some research on this subject I decided to give it the swerve. It is I believe, roughly in part, about inheriting trauma genetically from previous generations. I am not disputing it at all, I accept its validity. But do I need to involve it in my recovery? Does knowing about it help? Or does expanding my knowledge in this area and relating it to my healing process result in putting bricks in my kit bag in the form of complications I expend energy attempting to resolve, and end up carrying about…? My journey is about consciously lessening my load not adding to it. Again, it doesn't suit me but Epigenetics may well help others. However, I believe that childhood abuse was transmitted in my family line and I do add that towards a reason it happened to me. The 'cycle of abuse' which is about perpetuating learnt behavior, especially within a family, can exist and may be linked with Epigenetics, but I would say, although constricted by limited knowledge, they are not the same thing exactly. I can stop the cycle of abuse starting with an easy decision, but unraveling the implications of Epigenetics, for me, has too high an opportunity cost.

Bottom line? When it comes to books and help…you've got to kiss a few frogs. It's okay if the first few don't do it for you. And all the answers won't be in one book. And some books will contradict others. And some books, often written by therapists I find, will contradict themselves. And well, hold on, alternatively it could be….!

Books, obviously, are not the only vehicle for the written word. I read and write blogs, share emails, read articles on-line, send and receive emails, get info via social media, etc.

I feel we are in pioneering territory in terms of mental health, especially in the critical area of childhood abuse and, as such, a lot of relevant material doesn't make into books. And by the time a viewpoint makes it into a book (laborious, with time delay) it is old news or contradicted. Therefore, although I am anti 'social media' by way of a not too deeply considered prejudice, I do get a lot from on-line communication – shares from other folk especially.

I do recommend finding out about assertiveness training. Your trauma maybe caused by someone crossing your boundaries; inflicting their self upon you. If this happened during childhood it would be worth investing, as it is for a lot of us, in learning how to establish and enforce your boundaries in a way acceptable to society: learning how to say NO. I used to engage masculine presence bordering on intimidation, or caustic derisory wit, to enforce my boundaries with negative side effects. These methods are clumsy, often inappropriate and ineffective (longer term especially); I would find myself obsessing after an event, feeling shame for my behavior and frustration at the less than ideal external outcome.

Note: abuse and therefore trespass of boundaries can throw up a lifetime of vigilance for the survivor i.e. forever expecting and imagining that people have intruded physically or psychologically, and did so deliberately – this is not necessarily the case - people are just plain clumsy, they don't always think beyond the 'self', or anticipate your sensitivities. The survivor may also believe they have no right to enforce their own boundaries and by default invite invasion. In summary, learning some simple ways of saying 'No', and understanding it is okay to say 'No', is important. Easy for me to write but I understand it is not easy to do, but it helps if you are offered a path of useful techniques and phrases written in black and white – or go on a course.

4. Therapy

Fed-up one evening in the motel in an unfamiliar town Bob the traveling salesperson decides to have a 'mid-weeker' down the local. In the pub he gets chatting with a group of blokes having a couple after football training.

All is going well, 'I'll get these.' 'No, it's my shout, I'll get these,' and so on. They have a lot in common. After an hour or so Bob gets his John Thomas out and urinates over them all.

'Whhaaaattt!!' They stagger back in angry disbelief. One nearly punches Bob. But Bob is clearly distressed by his actions and is very apologetic.

'Oh no, oh no I am so, so sorry…' he goes on, clearly ashamed.

One of the men from the group takes Bob to one side.

'So, has this happened before?'

'Yes, a few times in fact,' says Bob looking at the ground, 'I feel terrible about it.'

The man gives him a card.

'Here, have a chat with this lady, she's a therapist. I've had my difficulties, but she's helped me.'

Six months later, same motel, same pub, same Bob, same blokes having a good night…

'I'll get these...', 'No, it's my shout, I'll get these...' and so on.

Then after awhile Bob gets JT out and urinates all over them again.

'Whhhaaattt!' exclaim the blokes angrily, obviously taken aback. One pulling back his fist prompting another to step in and stop him.

'Crying out loud mate didn't you speak to that lady?' said the one who gave Bob the card.

'Yes I did,' responds an upbeat Bob.

'So what happened?' the chap exclaims looking down at himself covered in urine.

'Yes, thank you for that, big help,' said Bob cheerily, 'I don't feel guilty at all!'

Therapy (I'll start again...)

Whooa....big one. Let me be clear, I have some strong views on therapy I am reasonably confident would march all over the accepted code by which therapists are supposed to adhere, and I will most probably upset or be disagreed with by some folk who've had therapy.

Point? Following are my opinions. They are only my viewpoints which relate to my journey only, but may be useful to you.

Also, please know for the record and judgment, I had just over two years of therapy with two therapists; one for a year followed immediately by a year with another, albeit I had therapy for a short period back in my late twenties some twenty five or so years ago.

I will stress up front, in balance, therapy is a good thing. In an ideal World everybody ought to at least try some and should have access to therapy as part of a health care process they can dip in and out of as they go, if they choose, through what has become a complex life for most of us which I reckon technology has made more so.

A continuous journey of self awareness *is the* way forward. It is our responsibility to continuously work on self awareness being the root to evolving positively as a collective which is vital given our increasing populous and ever reducing resource coupled with our existing prevalent pattern of World abuse. Maybe we are turning it around (focus on the positives!).

I would not be where I am today without therapy. There is a much higher probability I would have killed myself or still wrestling with addiction.

Talking therapy is said to actually change the neural routes. It can change you. It changed me – for the better. Many of the issues, ideas and techniques we discussed in therapy I refer to on a daily basis. To stop and really talk is hugely beneficial. Because of therapy life and being me is a lot easier, and more fun.

Therapy is not for everyone and if you can't get therapy or afford it, no problem. Believing you can't recover because you're not having therapy is a falsehood, potentially an excuse. People talk about waiting for therapy and in the interim put their recovery on hold; clinging on and waiting until the therapist rides in on the white horse to save them, potentially a recipe for disappointment having previously used the lack of therapy as an excuse not to recover, i.e. the long awaited therapy didn't work as hoped – now what? A feeling of desolation may ensue.

Another problem some face is having limited therapy e.g. being designated just ten sessions. This has the potential to leave them high and dry given therapy is about opening up which creates vulnerability. Feeling safe enough to disclose takes several sessions, and then it abruptly ends. Your car breaks down and the person fixing it takes out several parts from the engine then leaves the job half done. If offered just ten sessions, take them, but think of it as a supplement only, a springboard.

Therapy is just one tool in your kitbag, do other stuff too, or just do other stuff.

To put it in perspective, I believe a main purpose of therapy is to help the client develop mechanisms making navigation of life easier. Therapy is not an end in itself. Therapy won't take away your burden. Therapy is one vehicle by which you can explore your issue/s so you may face them and deal with them.

Good therapy employed by a client wanting to recover who is taking charge of their own recovery should, in my opinion, mean it ends. Effective therapy, I believe, should have an end point. The person is now equipped to get out and function in life. If not, doesn't it become therapy for the sake of therapy, for both parties?

I suspect that holding the belief the therapist is entirely responsible for one's recovery can become a trap e.g. going from therapist to therapist always dissatisfied.

'I've been divorced five times. I keep marrying the wrong type.'
Oh, it's about addiction to marriage.

Particularly, two candid books by ex-therapists I read claimed they need people to keep returning in order to have a steady income (the mustard company's profit is left on the plate). Submitting that some clients persist in trotting out the same stuff, narrating their last week, never committing to the responsibility, the self honesty, the stinging pain, that is part of moving on, getting through and recovering. What does a therapist do in these circumstances? Some I'm sure have integrity and will ask the client if 'it's working?' But how do they do this without making the client feel abandoned therefore worse?

My first therapist told me near the end of our time that she was advised by her support in the early period 'to throw me under the bus' (I get why now), but she toughed it out and that saved me.

I like to challenge myself and years ago I decided some years ago the scariest thing for me would be to sing in a musical, so I had singing lessons with that intention. I paid for and had the first round of ten lessons without practicing in between. Near the end of the last lesson I was all for having another ten and the subject of renewal came up after I had finished crooning and she, seated at the piano, stared up at me with concern in her eyes and said 'Hmmm...do you think you're getting any better?' and then folded her lips inwards...
So that was the end of my singing career. I actually had to get past deluded beliefs about my ability in the car on the way home, cursing out loud, 'ha, I'll show her...'. But she had integrity. She could have taken my money and to be frank, she looked like she could have used it.

An issue I have with therapy is that it is difficult to calibrate. What is success? When does it come? How is one to one therapy, where both parties are so personally invested, judged and measured by external objectivity such that it can be adjusted, if deemed necessary, to be effective and positive and avoid being damaging which it can easily be, or determined as stagnant? What a therapist says to a client can have resounding effects lasting a lifetime, and if negative or unhelpful can be difficult to dislodge given it comes from an 'expert who knows', the impact further enhanced by the client's vulnerable state; this happened to me.
I was and am aware that we had exacting terrain to cross but I would exit some early sessions feeling baffled and unsure whether I should or not. I was unaware of potential after effects, or that it was or wasn't okay to feel disturbed.

One way of immunizing oneself against potential harm is to filter what the therapist says, i.e. not fully take it fully on board. This potentially dilutes the good and possibly allows oneself to stay 'safe', or rather stuck in unhelpful patterns, as opposed to taking the risk required to question oneself, explore new ideas and ways of going through life.

I know therapists have a system of support, but what about a third party the client can check in with in order to take an objective view on the therapeutic process (rather than the specific content), given that the client is inexperienced and doesn't know what to expect, especially first timers, as to how therapy ought to be affecting them: an advocate for the client in relation to the therapeutic procedure perhaps? Every other service is subjected to customer/client feedback all except, I speculate, therapy, leaving room for incompetence which in such a sensitive an influential profession could be very dangerous.

Addictive too: it is very alluring having someone listen to you. I've been there, caught myself ranting on and telling anecdotes about unrelated stuff. Most people like being listened to especially once they know it is safe and without judgment. Being truly heard is a rare experience we all need. Similarly, being able to truly listen is a very rare and difficult skill.

Do the work – go in with intention. *Kid yourself? Why?*

My viewpoint has shifted given therapy helped me and I've witnessed it helping others. I had several therapy sessions which were permanently life changing for the better, they helped dislodge huge blocks in my mind I realized I held for years and never shared. But I have met a handful of people during the course of my life 'training to be counsellors' with unresolved issues I would condemn as serious and they don't seem to have the self awareness to confront them, and/or are taking psychotropic drugs [more], so are in effect diverting from their own issues (easier to solve other people's). For example, I read an in depth article concerning a therapist and author of a 'how to live your life' book (which I bought and read) who went on a World tour preaching his philosophy. Turns out he was addicted to psychotropic drugs and went on to have a break down, none of which appeared to be in any way his responsibility!

Does training to be a therapist occur to mentally healthy people? / Can a therapist experienced in resolving their own issues offer especially valuable help?

Therapists do not have a set prescribed formula just for you. I would be concerned if a therapist did think they were right and that 'this is the way forward'. I suggest you 'feel them out', get comfortable with the therapist therefore enabling you to share your deepest thoughts and related feelings. It takes a few sessions to build trust. Otherwise you might later sense the therapy isn't right for you and feel over exposed which may reverberate into a feeling of hopelessness, of being re-victimised: a sense of having thrown your soul into a hollow.

Give the relationship some time to settle and avoid judging too quickly. It's about balancing measured caution in order to build trust verses sharing and therefore making progress, or rather shelving the cynicism and getting on with it i.e. you can't build trust if you don't test it.

There is no set route. Best do what is best for you. I was compulsive and went in too deep before I had really tested the water. My lack of trust with everybody in general (see trauma list) later caught up with me and consequently I went through a phase of being destructive about the whole process i.e. pulling apart the therapist and her method or, according to my belief at that time, lack of it. I perceived I had shared too much with someone I didn't fully trust and felt shame at having allowed myself to become vulnerable, and subsequently converted the shame into cynical criticism.

Also note: The therapist is not a mind reader. You may think they know what you are feeling and thinking, but unless you tell them clearly they don't. Something I learnt in therapy is that I am not necessarily right about what other people are thinking, and they are not right about what I am thinking.

Looking back at my engagement with therapy I figured because I had 'fallen back' on 'help' for the first time in my life it would be waiting ready. The therapist would, and I believed should, know exactly what I needed and all I had to do was turn up, give a vague idea what was going on in my life and that would be that, the answers would appear, do ten or so sessions and that would be the end of it. But my expectancy of therapy did not match the reality. It wasn't about simply pulling into the pit stop and having a therapist fix things whilst I impatiently waited, then boot the accelerator and charge off back into life. Wrong: the therapist is the co-driver. They are there to help you navigate YOUR journey.

On that note, be ready for a false start with someone, and don't dwell on it. It's not you, it's the situation and the chemistry; you gave it a try and it didn't work so move on. Or, perhaps the 'professional' is just not very good at it, like any endeavor some will be rubbish. Although I hasten to add this caveat to what could be interpreted as negativity in some of the above: being a therapist is an occupation entered by fully considered conscious choice, taking a lot of study and dedication to qualify, and all those that register with a professional body adhere to a carefully considered code of practice. Those involved in the profession I hope and suggest, despite my cynicism, are dedicated to being the best they can be i.e. they have made a very specific considered choice – they ain't doing it by accident! I wrote an article and did a podcast for a therapy magazine and the unprompted responses I got from therapists glowed with incisive thought and care. But I still hold that there is room for incompetence.

From the off my second therapist 'had this'. I felt I could fall back and safe hands were there. She had a certainty and confidence given she had worked closely with a lot of male survivors of CSA, plus she spoke my code; she easily adapted her speech so that it matched mine. Notably though, she met me when I had traveled a long way already, rather than reacting like it was my first week of jungle warfare: I'd done a tour already and had honed tools and support. But with her experience came a tad of being tired with it all. *Been there myself in workaholic phases when I became competent and often reflected intolerance with others (previously a common theme with me + being shadowed by imposter syndrome): hard to keep things fresh.*

Maybe take into account 'modality' which I understand is something to do with the style of the therapy 'the school of thought'. I don't subscribe to the idea that modality is as significant as the proponent i.e. I think it boils down to the therapist, their personal style and the relationship with the client rather than the theory behind the therapy. I raised this point with a lady working right at the centre of the therapy trade and she said 'it was now a *spreading belief* this is the case' i.e. the success of the therapy depends more on the chemistry between the two people rather than the methodology.

So perhaps, when choosing a therapist, be only half interested in recommendations. Remember the taste in paintings analogy? A therapist who helped someone you may deem to be similar to yourself may not be right for you. And I would reserve the right to switch.

I also have a theory that people who are really good at stuff don't typically write about it. They would find it hard to explain, possibly because what they do has become part of their instinct which is difficult to translate to words: where knowledge and experience blend to become….intuition. A documentary about Japan focused on two beautiful septuagenarians that hunted for highly venomous sea snakes (10 times more so than rattle snakes) at night in caves. Standing in and snatching them from the water armed with only a linen bag to put them in, and when asked how they did it, given the snakes were so hard to see, without getting killed, one lady pondered and replied, '[she'd] been doing it for forty years and could just sense where they were, errrr it's….intuition'.

I read about a mock battle between sophisticated US fighter planes and primitive Russian MiGs during the cold war. The MiGs won because in the heat of battle the pilots couldn't manage all the complex controls of the US planes.

In parallel with the MiGs metaphor: an analogy I thought about is my sax playing. I improvise a lot. I have probably done nearly 10,000 hours of improvising. Every single piece of improvisation has been different, surely the same goes for therapy sessions; each and every one that ever was in the history of humankind is different. Not only that, I don't believe it would be possible for anyone to document any one of my improvisations using traditional musical notation such that another sax player, a better player than me (and I'm sure there are at least dozens in

London alone) could replicate exactly as I played by reading the music. Not given the myriad of variables including the make of sax, mouthpiece, reed, air pressure, temperature, air volume pushed through, environment, mistakes, my mood, the squawks, missed and flat notes (which I now consider as 'Kintsugi Improv' – embracing and recognizing the flaws as strength, character and real, earned, beauty).

The point: therapy is improvisation. To be a good improviser you need to have learnt the basics and be able to do the simple stuff well, and you need experience in improvising. The person who studied and learnt the most psychobabble will not necessarily be the best therapist. How many academics are good at actually achieving stuff other than academic stuff? To me the therapy business appears nestled in a lot of academic speculation and with that, contradiction. So what? Recruit the therapist that's read the most contradictions?

By the same token I wouldn't say the therapist with the most experience is *necessarily* the go to choice. Therapy itself is constantly evolving so a newly qualified therapist fresh with enthusiasm, idealism, the latest information may not be hamstrung by trying to fit your situation into a pattern they already understand, and so might be the best choice for you.

You will instinctively know the way. I am offering you some expectancy about how you might approach the engagement of therapy. There is no set right or wrong.

I went to the doctor with an arm problem and began to sob as I left and she asked if 'I wanted to talk to someone' (door knob consultancy – I think it is referred to as – severely inhibited by remote/on-line, appointments). I never cried and at 53 years of age I was weeping at any given moment. I decided I should give therapy a go. An experienced therapist was changing her modality and was regularly occupying a room at the surgery whilst helping a select number of people as part of her Masters degree.

The doctor offered me twenty sessions which I thought too many and figured I'd be fine after a few chats. After about the tenth I asked the therapist how many were left. The answer was good news and bad news in the same phrase.

'I've spoken to the doctor and she said you can have as many sessions as you need' (I had about 55).

It's going to take time, this Odyssey.

My advice in terms of qualifying a therapist would be to ask what experience they have of dealing with your symptoms. And perhaps, ask if they have experience in dealing with people with your background. The therapist needs to relate to your environment, your history, speak and understand your *code* (which you can be sure they won't have learnt from a lecture or book).

I regularly busk in an area of London that faces social challenges and sometimes intoxicated men (mostly) hover about. They want to get in my territory, my space, hang about and behave oddly. I am carrying a prized expensive saxophone so I am defensive and physically inhibited. At first it used to unnerve me because I wasn't sure how I should react to get the best result. Now I can pick them quickly and have already ***made the decision*** *that if they get in my space and physically touch me coupled with a threatening tone (as a survivor of an abusive household I am hyper vigilante and super sensitive to a threatening voice tone) then if a warning does not deter I will throw a* *right hook. Having made this decision i.e. that I have the right to defend myself and how I will enact this, I have certainty and by default I transmit confidence enabling me to address them gently and calmly without condescension, giving plenty of time and listening carefully without displaying any irritation. It always takes longer than I want but now I expect and allow for this, therefore defusing any intolerance. I treat them with respect and eventually I politely ask if they would mind if I carried on playing, they always comply often scratching around in their pockets for money in an appreciative fashion and they always depart without incident. They severely annoyed me at first, and then became a source of amusement, but now I empathise: what happened to this person such that they are drunk on cheap booze on a Tuesday afternoon? And believe me, once I treated them seriously with respect (they had obviously experienced so little) they mirrored me.*

From the first engagement you should sense the therapist is comfortable, at ease and confident. They are in control without being controlling. The drunk men no longer phase me at all, it's a given (and I hasten to add I haven't hit any). But the other day a gang of young girls aged about thirteen gathered round; they weren't being aggressive, but their energy! Frankly, I was terrified! If I was a therapist and a male client sobbed I'd be okay and able to give some positive help, but a teenage girl...if I said anything useful it would be an accident...

'...the therapist.... needs to speak and understand your code...'

I went into therapy believing the therapist would have all the answers. Part of me also believed I was an undiagnosed psychopath, or a similar label, and a potential danger to society. I suspected (*paranoia instilled by the anticipation of the childhood abuse)* she would be compelled to tell 'the authorities' and I would be extracted from society. I truly considered this to be an option (*another trait endured by many 'survivors' – that I was fundamentally 'different' & bad*). Also, I was ready to affirm a belief that all therapists were 'screwed up' and had also only ever led a life of academia which bore no relationship to mine, and consequently she was going to defile my mind. Plus, I couldn't readily access or share my feelings being an emotionally constipated middle aged man conditioned by my upbringing, peers and accepted 'role' (toxic masculinity). Add in that an abused child is conditioned to stifle their feelings by the perpetrators so as not to i) alert outsiders ii) cause the abusers to feel shame. So I thought expression of feelings was weak; an indulgence for others. I could not afford and should not have emotions so any vulnerability was surrounded by razor wire. But I was in a desperate state, crumbling fast and struggling to function at any level. I figured I probably needed to express my feelings but first I needed to engage them, and I had no idea what that involved until I met my first therapist.

What has my journey got to do with you? Only that yours will very probably be different so don't expect a pre-set journey as I did, I now realize. You are going into uncharted territory: the unacknowledged you. And remember, the therapist hasn't been there either! You are going off over that horizon (if you are to heal).

So, is the therapeutic process about looking backwards by way of gaining understanding of one's situation and issues, or is it about painting a picture of an alternative more positive view of the now coupled with a better perspective of the future? I discussed this concept with 'The Don' the other day and we were debating how much one needs to look in the rearview mirror (in a car, and therefore in life) by way of a parallel. One does, but all the time, how is that going to end?

A lot of psychobabble is conjecture. It is just theory. A lot of it gets very complicated which is alluring and easy to descend into. Psychology can be fascinating, but you and I want to recover. In depth understanding of one's well being, or not, via psychology offers rationale which aids acceptance. But I think there is a point where re-dissecting becomes self defeating if one is serious about living a full life: analysis paralysis i.e. a self absorbed journey up one's own arse, a trek I was on sometimes. I've heard talk of 'going through layers' which is true e.g. examine a primary like anger and it becomes, say, linked to shame, and then.... etc, etc, etc...but in the interim the cost can become not getting on with life by just keeping it simple. Complicating is not healing.

One can loose sight of the objective. Not see the wood for the trees.

Similarly, I am suspicious of 'labels' for 'conditions'. Understanding and dealing with issues on a cerebral level requires definitions, but can the label magnify an issue, 'I've been diagnosed with such and such, so that's me and I must carry on behaving in this way forever more'. The label becomes an excuse to avoid the onus of change, perhaps encouraging submission and entrapment to a way of being.

Therapy is about employing brutal self honesty which the therapist won't gift you, and their code won't allow them to apply the cold truth point blank. For example, at a homeless centre where I volunteered I met an ex-therapist who had taken a lower paid monotonous job after years of specializing in giving therapy to addicts. She said she was hamstrung by the fact she could not give it to them straight, "your addiction is your liability. Being an addict is your choice. I cannot *stop* you being an addict. Recovery is your responsibility." She told me she couldn't say this but wanted to, and so was forced to be patient, cajole and help them explore, etc, etc, and meanwhile they would go on and off the addiction until she gave up.

I've heard it said that some negative behaviors are justified because they are caused by trauma. Yes I get that, but once a client has identified the negative behavior, associated and accepted it is a result of the abuse/trauma then to continue the behavior, I think, is using the trauma as an excuse to avoid facing into it, taking responsibility and making the change. As an abuse/trauma survivor I emitted my abuse in a variety of ways as such you, I proffer, as a survivor will have done or do. The trauma you endured will leak out often in subtle ways, destructive to you and those around. I speculate that talking to the therapist can be rather like going to confessional whereby the 'sins' can be re-framed and made okay. The client can leave feeling okay but repeat the negative behavior alloyed with the excuse of being a trauma survivor, all enabled by the therapist making it okay again… this equals getting stuck (back to Bob).

An important part of having therapy is to understand and accept the therapist has ONLY a professional relationship with you limited to the period actually in the room. We should respect and understand there should be no emotional attachment. They owe professionalism according to their code of ethics but the relationship does not extend beyond that. That can make you feel abandoned and give the sense it is disingenuous, but better you go in knowing it will end, it should end, and the therapist will not be part of your everyday life going forward. Anything else is unhealthy for both parties.

Therapy is the support to life. Therapy is not the life.

Another question: male or female therapist? Odds are if you've no choice but are offered therapy, it will be a female. Why? Because there are way more female therapists than males = probability. Otherwise, it is entirely your call.

I perceived that both my female therapists were unsettled if I became overcome and tearful. Each time both would ask me questions part way through any outburst, therefore engaging my rationality. Asking a question can be a sobering antidote to an outburst of feelings. It felt inhibiting and it did re-invoke my shame for having feelings. I sensed they were not comfortable seeing 'a grown man cry'. I brought this up with my second therapist in the penultimate session when we were narrating the past journey and for the first time she was very defensive, like overly defensive, suggesting I was wrong.

I since had a wonderful weekend with a group of male CSA survivors facilitated by two male therapists very experienced in this arena. When any man sobbed (hand up) the facilitators sat in silence and waited; behavior we all naturally mimicked, for as long as it took for that man to go through it. The silent waiting felt respectful and supportive, and I discerned we as males found it easy to do. And I need to stress firmly here that contrary to what you may think, there was not a drip of discomfort among the men at witnessing another man cry, only respect and empathy.

Some months later a gaggle of brothers went on a walk around Dartmoor and we sat and read poetry (new concept for me) but by coincidence before the weekend I read some poetry and noticed it was better second time around. First time I found I was wrestling with the words, the nature of the poem, what it was trying to convey; like my mind was working on it in an analytical fashion. Second time I was able to feel the poem and enjoy it. My first year of therapy I wrestled with acceptance of my situation, I felt like everything was coming at me, often overwhelmed. The second lot, however, I chose how I wanted to view my situation and history. I was going into each session with *intention;* addressing a recurring pattern of behavior and thought process or, less often, an event that happened in the last week to which I reacted incongruently (triggered) thereby offering a window to a deeper issue I wasn't recognizing or dealing with.

Getting below the surface is the route to healing.

If you are not using therapy as a tool to 'dig into' yourself, then it's no good moaning about it, or having it, in my opinion.

'Do you think you're improving?' asked the singing teacher... '...because you might if you practiced, because just now you're wasting your time and mine. And you're not going to change because I've asked if you practiced several times and you always make a disdainful joke about it because you're paying you think you're entitled and that I can't criticize you. But I'm not going to sit here and sacrifice my integrity by listening to your never improving screeching anymore. Just coming here is not going to make you a good singer, so let's call it quits, shove your

money, we both deserve better; well I certainly do. You can take your delusion elsewhere!' she thought.

It's worth noting that whatever the style of therapy with whomever, it will most probably have a ceiling of use and ability. Be prepared to be disappointed if you are expecting therapy to be the only thing you need. I doubt it will. Perhaps a reason why some people keep going back is they are trying to squeeze something out that isn't there. And your journey will be different to mine. I offer stuff about mine by way of expressing it is far from being an exact. It is too complex for that to be possible.

In summary.
Have therapy. But try and qualify it in advance: their experience and the style.
Establish trust and boundaries.
Feel comfortable? Get in there – do the work. Growth requires **you** to push at your edges and go beyond.
I am deeply *grateful* to both therapists.

'I quit therapy because my analyst was trying to help me behind my back'

Richard Lewis

5. Group Work – sharing

'If you want to go fast, go alone. If you want to go far, go in a group.'

The book I read six times by a therapist who is very experienced in helping male CSA survivors is a massive advocate of group therapy, over and above one on one therapy (I think it is fair to say). Conversely, I mentioned to my first therapist that I had begun attending group therapy meetings and she 'had mixed views', I read 'skeptical'.

I am an advocate but I understand the skepticism.

I just stopped and thought for a while. If I had only one tool/method at hand to help me recover, what would it be? Would it be group work? I give a hesitant 'could well be'. I found it to be powerful and healing, but it is a malleable vehicle, groups differ in nature and change as time goes on i.e. people come and go, altering the dynamic. I often think, 'right that's it I am done with this group…' but my blueprint laid out five or so years ago was 'I am going to recover' and with that one of the main edicts of the first group I went to was, 'keep coming back,' so generally I do and, for sure, the next I attend I will experience an enlightening revelation. As a result I have made connections with people on an emotional and spiritual level I have rarely experienced. I've heard words to the effect that they [a participant] only feel as though communication within the group matters and that all else is superficial, I get that.

For example, one of the deepest bonds, of the many I made, was with a young lady aged about twenty three that happened to be black and happened to be a lesbian and our Worlds could not have been more different (musical tastes, hobbies, interests, history, ambitions, etc, etc) but it felt like we had been on the planet as great friends in a previous life where maybe I was a much younger female and she was an older male: the 'labels', 'differences', 'genders', blah, did not register. The connections you make transcend all the usual social conditioning nonsense, and with that you can plug your spirit into the continuum of humanity.

Going to group therapy affected my life profoundly. I gifted me the possibility to make truthful and sincere connections with others. Humans are cloaked in many guises but I grasped we share a commonality no matter what shell our spirit inhabits.

We are social creatures. We seek each others' company. People naturally gravitate to each other. I could waffle on about the psychology of the clustering of people which I have studied in considerable depth, evidenced in cinemas, queues, doing the same thing, buying the same things. It is important for trauma survivors to know there are people enduring or have lived through, the same stuff as you, and they will offer ways to *keep moving*. Sharing your stuff is very important. Listening to others sharing their stuff is very important. You can learn so, so much on several dimensions.

I've lived in different countries and done a ton of different jobs, done a ton of different things, some I won't commit to ink right now, and thought I knew people. I thought I knew me. I thought I understood what humanity was. I thought I'd heard it all. I thought I knew how close people could get i.e. not very close. I thought I understood that there were 'types' that behaved in a given way, and that I'd met them all. I got into group therapy and found I was wrong about all of the above.

But it is not for everyone. And again, if you can't access relevant group therapy, no sweat: it is just another tool, all of which overlap.

Like therapy, know that each group will be different in nature. Be aware of being quick to judge if your first sessions leave you wanting.

If you've not tried groups let me, if I may, get you 'Aldo'd up' – give you some expectancy.

Know this: some people keep going back to the group and see it is as a life support system. Whereas others want to leave half way through their first meeting and never go back, or alternatively, give it a fair trial but find it is not for them. All good. Whatever suits you.

Largely, groups have a theme. The 12 step programme for Alchoholics Anonymous is one, obviously, it is for alcohol addicts. A now close friend and survivor whom I made a fantastic connection with on my journey (one of the angels that appeared in my life), attended MAA (Marijuana Addicts Anonymous) meetings in a disciplined fashion. And I have attended a group based around the 12 steps programme adapted for CSA survivors which I did for eighteen months, including a spell chairing/facilitating it. I am now a semi active member of two other groups.

Going to a new group can be foreboding. Again, I was very skeptical. Before my breakdown I would've sneered at the concept of group therapy but as I unraveled I needed all the help I could get, despite the act of reaching out being a big move for me but I figured I should put aside my closed mind as it may inhibit my recovery, and I was right to do so…but….

Walking into my first meeting was like broadcasting a confession: I need help, I am weak, I am not 'normal', I am not functioning. I felt I was betraying myself and giving license to strangers to judge me. I felt vulnerable and was therefore defensive.

Joining a group is a process that may not conform exactly to your ideal. Even if you think you hadn't created any pre-conceived ideas – you will - and it's worth being aware of this, otherwise the first handful of meetings might at times feel bruising. When you first engage you will be alert and sensitive, your 'oh well, it doesn't matter' filter will be switched off. Everything will matter, like anything new you join in with, especially when the other people are familiar with procedures and each other. It is 'normal' to feel sensitive, which is acutely enhanced in group therapy involving deep personal issues such as addiction or abuse.

My second ever meeting started in café before the official session in the church hall. The café meet wasn't obligatory but I went along. The lady that ran the group, a fellow CSA survivor – it was survivors only – not a trained therapist just one of the group, made the casual comment after I ordered a cup of tea (English breakfast), 'What? Who drinks tea?' with, I perceived, a tone of condescension – *(I believe around 100 million cups a day in the UK)*.

All sorts of thoughts went racing into my head about how she was undermining me, triggered by the fact that 'the father' specialized in this activity (projecting his own insecurity)…plus other stuff, breach of boundaries/judgment, etc, etc, and I had an internal explosion and couldn't speak. I went back to her later with this issue; she was very apologetic and understanding. I realized it was no big deal, just a throw away comment and any other time I would have seen it thus. *Part of my growth and healing is in looking to forgive people as they did not abuse me during my childhood - not attach the feeling of being a victim to every perceived slight against me, and so building resilience.* We became friends and bonded, and like several people I've met in 'group', grew love and respect for her. She had a condition caused by the abuse she suffered as a child and a few months later it was a contributory factor in her sudden death.

The group has since dissipated I believe, but I still do go through fits and starts with the 12 steps. The World would be a better place, in my opinion, if everybody did a form of them. A concept several would disagree with… I accept their viewpoint….its the 'submission to 'God & a higher power' I know some don't like – I didn't much at first either [more].

Via a consenting email thing a bunch of brother's share, I recall one venting about how he was treated badly on his first visit to a group, and thereby criticizing the structure and process. I could relate to his frustration knowing if it were me a handful of years before I would be obsessing about going back armed with a flame thrower! I did empathise: yes, they were wrong, but by way of gaining movement on the issue it's worth stepping away and considering your own position which is exaggerated by the circumstances, your feelings, and perhaps, an unrealistic expectancy. The people there are doing their best. They are trying to do a good thing but have their own stuff going on which is consuming them in a big way, leaving little room to imagine what you are going through. They are just people. They are not the abusers. Let go of impulse to attach past abuse to this/a situation.

It is likely you'll need to attend a few meets before you settle in. Other group members will share banter before and after the group, and most probably will be, should be, at ease with each other. This will feel intimidating and a little exclusive. At my first group sessions I often regressed back to my childhood, adopting a feeling of not being part of what was happening, sitting alone in wet pants threading beads alone inside at school whilst the others played outside. *I was being abused at home (I pray that if a teacher sees a six year old behaving like this they suspect immediately the child is being abused – I fear not though – we've so, so much work to do – all of us – 'it takes a village to raise a child' – we are all responsible for every child*). But, by the same token, it would be fair to welcome you to the group. That is not a 'hallelujah it's you!' Just an easy 'slide your self in here'.

Some groups are facilitated by trained counsellors and others are run by attendees as per their agreement. My preference? Neither. They are different and serve a purpose. Given the choice if you are new to groups, go to one facilitated by a trained person. The fundamentals behind the purpose and code of group therapy is to allow people to express themselves and listen to others in an equal, non-threatening, non-judgmental, and mutually respectful environment. A trained facilitator should be able to oversee and implement this process, and could well steer the group by helping to address specific issues thereby aiding recovery i.e. highlight a theme for each session. A facilitator led group should, to a large extent, follow the same procedure each session. Peer led groups will wobble more, being dependent on who attends i.e. they are more easily influenced by the group dynamic.

Any group should have a format of some sort which I believe ought to be written down for reference and all attendees should be aware of it, and agree to abide by the rules and guidelines. In my experience without structure the group loses focus and can easily become destructive for attendees, leaving the 'process' prone to abuse most likely in some form of judgment (even seemingly trivial like appearances e.g. 'oh you look ..... tonight' - NO), albeit unwitting.

I personally benefit most from a prescriptive approach to group therapy. I visited a charity managed by survivors of childhood abuse that offers a programme of recovery via group work and engages a fixed approach for survivors, even giving homework. They explained the philosophy which made sense to me. Depends, again, what suits, some just want to get together and have chat. Good, much better than not.

To this day I would like to thank with heartfelt sincerity the lady that adapted the original AA 12 steps for CSA survivors to follow. I liken them to a rope I could pull on to drag myself out of the swamp. I have been through them eight times so far (with the group & alone). We took turns to run the weekly group and in the eighteen months I attended lots of different people came and went; we oscillated in numbers from three to twelve. I did a step each week and talked about what I had learnt. Mostly, others chatted about issues in their life, or historic stuff. Only I stuck to the programme consistently. It took me an age to accept that the others didn't choose to do the steps; I thought they were missing the point, that I was right and they were wrong. I was right, but I was wrong to think they were wrong. I happen to like the directive approach, a roadmap. Having the steps gave me the choice to be proactive with my recovery; I could proactively remedy the effects of trauma.

A key feature of the 12 steps is the challenge of engaging pure self-honesty which stings, but this is where growth occurs in my opinion. Paradoxically, a big lesson I learnt is, growth also occurs by letting go and going along with the flow i.e. being flexible and open rather than rigid e.g. accepting the others not doing the 12 steps!

Each member should be allowed the same amount of air time. At my first group time was not managed and I figured this was how groups were. It was a case of speak if you want to for as long as you like. Unregulated, some dominated and resorted to the familiarity of repetition because it is safe (we all obsess to some degree or other). Arguably they are stuck or, another view is, they needed to go through this iterative process, if they ever do; hey, it is their way and therefore their journey, but the price was paid by the quieter folk because vocal attendees would happily soak all the time without a thought. In summary, I like the idea of having strict time keeping. And importantly, any group should be about equality with no hierarchy.

It is likely that facilitated groups (by a trained person) have an 'air time' control feature and similarly, encourage the quieter ones to say their piece. That said there is a feeling of being monitored and judged by the facilitator which can generate thoughts and behaviors i.e. an 'authority figure' instigates reactions/conformity to a belief system, or is that just me? Let's not go there, it gets too complex. But I do know that some facilitated groups will prompt participants to say stuff that aligns with a known philosophy of the facilitator: looking for approval.

There is something wonderful about a group having an agreed system of being led in turns by one of the attendees. The group develops its own journey as it evolves. It becomes a story in its own right.

Going to 'group' is analogous. It will have a beat: a life of its own. But know it is possible a group you take part in will end, or you will chose to stop going. That's ok. Even now as I edit I suspect my involvement with groups will lessen. I met a survivor friend of mine recently to compare notes and he described going to group/s as a 'phase'.

The power of the truths, the suffering endured, the injustice, the triumphs, the pain, the love, the stories I have heard, the shear force of humanity has many times, brought me to tears: tears of sadness and of joy; tears through being so fervently connected to humanity. No drug will match it.

One on one therapy helped me look at myself and life in an expanded way; group therapy helped me find a deep connection with and regain faith in humanity.

Groups taught me to trust.

Isolation (loneliness) is one of the biggest killers. We are all influenced by those around us. It makes sense to heal in a group. There is enormous healing effect in meeting others enduring the same issues as you, and an important first rule of recovery is DO NOT ISOLATE! Let's note: people do not, generally, kill themselves in the company of others. It is easy to be seduced by the allure of being alone especially when we feel low, but we must be aware if we are always choosing by default to be alone - not good. We must consciously observe that inner chattering monkey and be aware if it is forever telling us to stay away. Being alone most of the time, for the majority of us, is mentally unhealthy. There is good reason why solitary confinement is a punishment.

Another point to consider, especially poignant for survivors of familial childhood abuse be it physical, emotional, psychological or sexual; a group can be a surrogate family. It was for me, providing the support I never had. It gives me a sense of belonging. A group of male survivors of CSA I am proud to be a part of refer, by choice, to each other as 'brothers'. I have a group of 'brothers' close by, I often feel tearful with love when I think of them. You can't buy that, it is precious. The feeling of isolation and of being alone with my troubles has gone. I just sat back and realized that. I had to think my way back to how I used to think and that I couldn't share how I felt; I couldn't express the darkness within to others. I always maintained a 'front', kept wearing the mask, and only engaged other people using the code I believe they expected of me. I know many people feel like this. It cripples until you hit a point when you have to talk. Believe me, to share with others who understand and believe you, to hear others speak their truth you recognize within yourself, is spiritually restorative.

My deepest darkest patch lasted for over nine months when it was easier and better if I stayed home; safer for me and others since I was swaying between forlorn little boy to being consumed by fierce anger which could easily have manifested physically. My default was to curl up and hide away which I did, both a functional practice and necessary. By contrast, again paradoxically, to recover rather than slide towards suicide I needed to push myself to interact. I needed an environment where I would be safe both physically and spiritually. Going to group therapy each week gave me that.

I recommend you, as a trauma survivor, do the same.

My guess is you will change your judgment of others in the group as it unfolds in front of you. Going to 'group' taught me not to hold on to judgment, and that I could change my judgment, and if didn't latch onto the first one too tightly it would change quickly anyway. Then I learnt not to judge.

I attended a seminar thing on racism: how to recognize it and defuse it, at my local council in an area of London which is multi everybody from everywhere. I happened to be the only white middle aged man in the group attended by a healthy mix of people. I thought I would get a roasting given I always believed that 'we' are associated with 'the system', 'the establishment', 'prejudice', 'privilege', 'misogyny' …and whole bunch of other not too positive stuff. The first thing the lady who facilitated the meeting said, which came as a surprise i.e. it was a surprise she just said it, was that we all have the potential to be racist: it can be a natural response to have a negative judgmental possibly racist (among others) thought when someone that looks different to you does something that misaligns with your view. But it's what you choose to think next that's important. It's natural to put people into categories and stereotype people, a reflex reaction helping us feel safe because we think we know and understand them. Group therapy teaches to take the next step, to consciously recognize you have made a wrong judgment and to let go, to view it for what it was, a knee jerk safety driven first reaction.

At the seminar we candidly shared our first thoughts on how the others would judge ourselves, and we were all way wrong! People don't judge you anywhere near as much as you judge yourself. They are less bothered about what you project than you think, certainly not as much as you are.....But never mind, for us the point is: be aware of judgment. Vocalizing judgments in groups has to be stopped. People should just talk about themselves. Similarly, this crosses into giving advice, no thank you, stay in your lane. I have been in group meetings (the self regulating variety) where one member has chosen to give advice '..what *you should* be doing…'. I have, at times, felt compelled to do this but refrained. I have previously given advice albeit from a standpoint of 'what I have found/ what has helped me…', but perhaps with the intention of transmitting '..what you should do…'. Unraveling where this need to give advice comes from can become complex, but advice and judgment is best avoided, it may not be received in the spirit it was offered. And if offered, just say 'No thank you, your advice is not invited.'

Be wary of the person taking on the role of pseudo psychotherapist and becoming controlling; it becomes about them, conveying their abuse by manipulating others into seeking their approval whilst avoiding their own issues. I twice re-visited the group I first attended after a long break; it had changed personnel along with the tone. On my first revisit there was a strong minded articulate lady running the group (not a qualified therapist/counselor) and had been for sometime (it is healthier, I believe, for members to take turns), and outsiders were obviously viewed by her as a threat. After each person spoke she, unprompted, gave her advice… 'I think what you should be doing..', if this happening – exit stage left.

I joined a group which was highly vetted. There are strict guidelines about sticking to 'I' statements in 'shares' (group parlance for speaking out) rather than 'you', so what is said is purely about the speaker, even to the point of not using labels for the other members 'mate, brother, …' etc. In my view anything other than this methodology potentially disables a member from feeling totally safe and able to uninhibitedly express. Anything less can, even at an unconscious level, create the need for conformity to a perceived code therefore the need for approval from the group or specific members.

Another basic, (this is a street fighting aspect of recovery and group therapy), what happens between group sessions between members? Among my closest relationships are with group members but (there is a serious 'but' here) I have stayed close to three people from my first group and each of us had difficulties with one or more members outside the meetings.

You may want to help others. I think this is a healthy thing to do (important caveat: when you are ready – you will know). Frankly, I am suspicious of those in 'recovery' after many years of therapy that do not reach out to help others: it is still all about them. I recall reading a book by an ex-therapist who was of the opinion that some people you can't help; they don't want to change, skilled in living off the goodwill and spirit of others. There is no doubt a few trauma survivors become like this and are deft at drawing you in and exploiting you, so beware the emotional vampires.

An observation: In relation to me supporting two men that were struggling. I noticed an odd 'man thing' that took some working out. They'd start opening up after some patience on my part (new). And once they felt better after a few chats/tears they wouldn't be grateful, no, the opposite. They would avoid me, fine, or be disdainful and employ 'tough guy' mockery (push me away). It cost a friendship in one case and it was him that kept calling me when he was struggling. I eventually figured that perhaps they were ashamed of having shown vulnerability and I now reflected/symbolised the weakness they had displayed. Their silly toxic masculine armour was now back on! A bit like I was with my first therapist. Oh dear men, we're trapped!

You will hopefully find the expression of your troubles very helpful and form connections and go on to give folk your number; feel robust enough to help others, as I did. I gave mine to a chap who appeared to be struggling having just joined the group. I hate the idea that people are going through what I did with so little support and understanding. I was seasoned enough to tell him my number was not for general chit chat, rather when the dark cloud was looming and he needed help, and that I only take calls on Monday through to Friday nine until five, beyond these times my phone is usually off, but I promised I regularly check my messages and would call him back within twenty four hours. I know well when the suicide python wraps around the feeling of reaching out and nothing happens: you need expectancy about support i.e. you need to know it is definitely out there and when it will engage.

My phone soon started ringing. It was him. I was busy the first time, eating in café (a proper one with big plastic tomatoes on the tables) as it happened (just about to gorge in to a full English – my guilty pleasure – wife a veggy!). No problem I was alone, no one around, my food would go cold but I could live with this (almost). My heart raced somewhat because I needed to concentrate, really listen and pick my words carefully. A phone conversation where such a lot is at stake takes serious concentration. He chatted and chatted about general stuff. He did all the talking about him and notably didn't ask anything about me, further notably, didn't ask whether or not it was convenient for me to listen to him talk *at* me. I thought he was rambling by way of release so I let it go, let him talk. But it went on for over half an hour and he seemed okay, he just moaned. I had to cut in and gently stop him, and afterwards my meal was cold and I sat trying to work out what had happened. Had I missed something? Then he called again and again, day after day, often outside of the allotted hours and therefore leaving messages, he even caught me with my phone on at nine at night with my dinner on my lap watching TV with my wife. I left my food once more and went into another room, heart racing on yellow alert, and he unloaded again. He called twice more and then I told him firmly not to contact me again. In essence, he was passing on his abuse by being abusive. People do this; I believe we all do in various ways but we don't realize it.

Similarly, a male friend from the same group left and went back when I wasn't attending anymore and apparently had a difficulty with a chap during this period. He didn't share the detail but he eventually stopped going to the group because of it. Similarly, a female friend had a member infiltrate her life and visit her at home; he became controlling and intimidating.

So, hand out your number only to people with whom you've shared several sessions and feel comfortable with, and I urge you to consider putting in boundaries. Otherwise, the default is: don't give your contact details. You may be in a vulnerable state so play safe. Or, you may think you are in a strong place and can be supportive, but find later you are not; your journey changes and becomes overwhelming, then you are not helping yourself or them. My friend, who had the problem I mentioned, expressed this same viewpoint: he thought he was okay when he offered support but he went off the track himself and couldn't cope with the extra burden of another's troubles, especially someone being destructive. You may be inviting a problem person into your life you think you are equipped to handle, but you are not. Remember, beware the emotional vampires, they come well disguised. Therapists rarely go around giving their home phone number for good reason.

Let's remember all is based on my experience viewed through my lens. In balance, I recommend you go into group therapy with a discerning attitude. Maybe qualify it first, as they ought to qualify you by way of protecting existing members/ explain agreed boundaries. And give the group the benefit of the doubt, particularly in the early stages. The first time I heard others share their stories I felt like I had walked alone across a desert and flopped into an oasis of cool fresh water. To know you are not alone can be heartbreaking but contrarily, you will share a commonality that is healing. To this day the band of brothers (now named 'The Trust Brothers') I am proud to be a part of, share, support, educate, sympathize, understand, and love unconditionally.

One of the brothers put the question out there (and invited responses)...
'...I've been through this huge arc of recovery that has soaked up so much of me and my life, it has caused me to go through and back through stuff that is so hard...and now feeling as though I have recovered and find life is a lot more simple...what have I got? Is it part of abuse to find yourself having wasted so much of your life?'

{these are my words/interpretation of what he said}

I did attempt a response….it was about how we wouldn't inflict abuse and so the trauma on anyone, and we wouldn't want anyone to go through the Odyssey of recovery. But the journey brings an understanding and empathy with humanity others often never achieve. I believe this can be found through group therapy, and it is one of only a few ways.

6. Support Network

An important addendum to all of the above about 'group' is this –
Think about building a network of people you can call on. I am going to talk more about this in conjunction with 'Declaration' i.e. 'I am in this state; this is what happened to me.'

How you and I view ourselves in terms of how we interact with others varies. How we behave changes dependent upon the person we are with and the circumstances. You may see yourself as a loner for example, an attention seeking extrovert, oscillating within, or capable of both in an extreme fashion, either way although interaction with others is on occasion bruising in order to recover acquiring a support network will help. Again, people generally don't commit suicide in the company of others. Forming a support network is another foundation stone; its size and nature is inconsequential, and there is no right or wrong about this, it doesn't bear comparison, but let it become a default. Let me tell you in black and white that having folk around to share with is very helpful, in balance. I say 'in balance' because there is a 'feet up' here i.e. a need to look ahead and create an expectancy by way of preventing you from catastrophising when you feel the support is not there. Or, more specifically, when people you expected to support you turn into chocolate soldiers when the heat is on.

A formal 'group' can be a great source of people to add to your support network. Contact outside of the group may be prohibited which should be respected. Otherwise, I discovered having the phone number of someone is reassuring. It gives me the option. If I go into a dark cloud I know people who've been there and understand. Group people are linked beyond the social conditioning typically included in relationships e.g. status, age, etc. And it is unlikely you will share any history with them and so the code of your communication is based purely on the mandate created by the group. I have friendships with group members I've held for sometime with no idea where they live, their occupation, hobbies or if in a relationship. These factors are important when forming connections 'out there in the World' but become insignificant, unless part of an issue a member is tackling, among the group. It helps having people uninvolved in your everyday life you can turn to; it keeps their view objective and enables open communication.

I am a firm believer in the '....want to go far, go in a group' ideology. In my observation, folk that recover the best i.e. don't sink back into depression so easily and have, as one brother put it, 'big patches of calm that seem to be getting bigger', and another 'wonder if I should feel guilty because I feel okay about myself and everything', are the folk persisting with a group. Plus especially, they help and do things beyond just themselves. They actively get out and speak out, campaign for the greater good, facilitate groups, share information, write stuff, attend meetings, and significantly are there for others i.e. they form a network of people that they actively help. Their recovery is not just about them.

You want to help yourself then help others.

Align yourself with people like this. More equals more. Your peers have an appreciable influence on your life. My network is growing. I recently connected with a well traveled wonderfully inspiring group of sisters stopping domestic abuse, and are bringing to light and halting abuse of females on college campus where the rape statistics are seriously troubling.

Note: a support network is like a garden: it takes constant tending, care and input. You'll get out what you put in. Some folk will wilt out of your life but keep planting seeds with others and nurture folk, support them and in turn they will nurture and support you.

7. Body work

Right from the off I will state my belief. I reckon in the not too distant future main stream medical professionals will recognize that healing from trauma will primarily be about banishing it from the body.

Trauma is held in the body; to heal you need to get it out. That is my firm opinion based on the experience of my journey and an opinion mirrored by people with qualifications if that's the reassurance you need.

Understanding trauma and its effects on behavior can spiral in complexity. There is a lot of psychotherapy stuff out there, tons of it. You can follow threads of theories, research, ideas, beliefs and statistics etc, into various avenues, but in the depths of depression theories and books may have limited use. I often struggle to understand the psychobabble language they are written in, sometimes they do make for fascinating reading and discussion, but as to practical use…?!

If you find a therapy book among the crash debris when washed up on the hostile island, great - useful for kindling.

When struggling in a state of crisis you need direct action. You need to stem the bleeding. Theoretical waffle offers limited help; I know I've been there. When my breakdown started I knew I was in serious trouble when my life, my thoughts and feelings descended into territory I had no experience of. What didn't help was finding when I did get help it contained, and seemed built around, the word 'existential'.

In the next 24 hours in all the hospitals, building sites, restaurant kitchens, farms, factories, war zones in the whole World i.e. environments where action is required, I'll bet not one person will say in any language the word 'existential'. In fact, I've investigated 'existential' in some depth and still have no idea what it is – I'm calling bluff on this one – I don't think anyone does, they only pretend they do.

We all have a stack in which the stress we experience gets poured. Some have a bigger stack than others. I heard one can increase its depth by gradually taking on more and more stress. For the trauma survivor a massive amount of stress got dumped into the stack, anymore pours over the top causing less than useful thoughts and behaviors (hysteria/chaotic). Conversely, in times of high stress many survivors perform well; accustomed to extremities they are able to disassociate therefore preventing feeling overwhelmed and so reacting with rational calm. I recall reading that we make good ambulance drivers.

There are chemical reactions in the mind and body that stress initiates. It is about adrenaline and cortisol; they prepare the body for fight or flight (there are several books/documents on this subject), an influx causes the body to tense up. Survivors of trauma are often hyper alert to danger or, moreover, are susceptible to perceived danger i.e. we see danger where it doesn't exist. This equals tension in the body, tension pulsing into the body and not passing through i.e. being ingested instead.

I went to yoga classes in Auckland back in the late 80's led by a chap that had lived in India and studied under B. K. S. Iyengar (there's a lot, a lot to Yoga from what little I know I don't know). This chap did know. We were in a pose and he claimed as one releases knots in the body, memories visit: memories of how the knots were caused.

Not long after in a stretch digging into a knot in my shoulder, I was transported to a moment when I was a boy. The memory was clear and consumed all of me. I used to climb trees a lot; we had some in our garden. I was up the apple tree which was a bit awkward to scale. I felt my weight go backwards as my foot slipped; one hand was free and I stretched for the branch but it seemed to move upwards and shrink and I instantly felt a hollowness in my stomach and sense of weightlessness, an age passed when I observed the recognition and acceptance I was falling, seeing the sunshine through the branches, the smells of a spring day, the sound of the breeze through the budding leaves and thinking 'this is a long fall, I am going to hit the ground hard, I wonder how hard it will be?'

More recently (pre lock down) at my Yoga class the wonderful Donna (who also knows what she is talking about) said repeated tension gets stored in the fascia (a complex network of fiber attaching muscle to bone – which makes sense). Flinching regularly causes muscles to contract which eventually translates into an abiding state in the fascia i.e. the constant tensing of the muscles keeps pulling on the fascia and tightens it permanently thus contorting the skeleton, and this takes applied effort over a long period to expel. As I understand it – I know little of physiology.

For most of my teenage and adult life I have had a duodenal ulcer and subsequent knot of pain in my abdomen, plus an on going problem in the small of my back such that 'they' were talking about fusing my discs together despite countless visits to chiropractors (*notably: I was in traction when I was nineteen for three weeks – the 'specialists' believed this was the cure, it achieved only my gaining weight – glad I didn't tell them I was getting headaches and depressed, 'soon have you sorted, I'll ask nurse to fetch the drill from the cupboard'...!*), also a constant ache in my shoulder blade, and on-going irritable bowel syndrome. They are all gone now. My posture at 58 is better than ever. I feel physically powerful given the fluidity of my body, and without regularly eating fiber I become constipated which I would never have believed possible (we'll stop there on that one, thank you). I am chilled inside rather than constantly angst. Oh, it feels so good.

Yes, the talk therapy helped but it was the body work, exiling the trauma from my body, that brought a large portion of these positive results, affecting the way I think and behave. It is a bit 'chicken and egg' though – bodywork vs talk therapy in terms of whether or not one needs the talk therapy before you can just delve into the bodywork for it to be effective. I would suggest not. In fact, I would go as far to say that bodywork is more effective than talk therapy and given the option of only one I would go with body work and ditch the psycho existentialism. But contradictorily (I'm allowed), being armed with therapeutic theory does help the cognitive processing of feelings when they come up.

Bodywork in relation to dealing with trauma is relatively new and I get the impression that some talk therapy exponents are suspicious (threatened?).

I watched a clip of film featuring a CA survivor & now psychotherapist who has done a mountain of great work in the area of CA, citing how animals shake when they are stressed. They shake it out. And he talked about how he was triggered and processed an episode of shaking; it took a month to work through. I got the feeling bodywork was a revelation for him in terms of his journey, and the theory behind it. Unfortunately, this part of his story was given much air time, but I have since seen more recent stuff of his which majors on the relationship between trauma and the body.

It is given that yawning vents tension and therefore contributes to dismissing trauma from the body. It was highlighted by the man 'that knows' at the survivors weekend that many of us would repeatedly yawn. We did.

'If you want to help yourself, help others.'

My wife would say this on occasion during my breakdown, so I took it on board and volunteered at some local homeless centres. I became the cook at one and had an 'Indian lavatory' equivalent experience, which is to say I ended up in a corridor on the floor in the fetal position convulsing violently and yowling until physically and spiritually exhausted [I will revisit this one – see chapter on Fear]. In summary, I expulsed a boulder of fear created and held in my body from my childhood that had continually permeated my life, my being, my everyday.

As my first therapist taught me; you need to sit in your pain. You need to be with it, accept it, and enable it to consume you. You may well sob and shake, but you must midwife yourself through it, hold yourself in and through it, be with it, and that is the only way you will expel it.
(The most important advice in this book)

Don't get me wrong; I wasn't totally cleansed after 'the corridor' experience, not by a good margin. The release of the bulk of the fear and hopelessness from my core was a big shift but the residue took months to flush out. During the early stage of my recovery I went to bed every afternoon at about 3pm, curled up with a couple of teddies and regressed to my childhood and sobbed and shook and slept a couple of hours for a total of around nine months. The rational part of me figured I may have to accept this as a permanent condition and I would have to engineer a life involving going to bed every afternoon and sobbing, like living with a permanent disability. Not so. It passed.

I have a 'back rack'. A wooden foot wide bow with the apex a quarter of the way along and pairs of wheels down its one metre length. I lie on it with the apex pressed into the middle of my shoulder blades. I decided previously to dig into my shoulders and neck. In profile I used to stand slouched with my head forwards and neck curved. Tension stored in my fascia had disfigured my posture given a lifetime of flinching; add in shame, guilt and lack of self worth. I spent over a year lying on this contraption daily for an hour focusing on my spine and all the accompanying muscles. Like yoga it requires I sit at the 'edge': the pain frontier, breathe mindfully and be patient waiting for the softening.

On the 'rack' recently I was transported to a series of memories around the same event. When I was seven I became overwhelmed in class and began to cry quietly when we were supposed to doing a written exercise. It took me sometime recently to associate the crying in class event with being sexually abused at the swimming baths by a stranger. I now realized I had, as a small boy, subsequently developed a sense that my home, where I was abused, was not safe and neither was the World.

I'd catch a bus into town, meet a friend and we'd walk through a dangerous part of the city to go swimming. We'd overstay because we'd learnt how to cheat the time system and I would get back to an often empty house, at no agreed time, aged seven. Abusers can pick neglected children, hence being manipulated by a friendly man in the shallow end. There were at least six boys that he was frolicking with earlier and I wonder if they had also been encouraged to play 'the tickling game' alone with him. It was a routine for him. Weekly? For how long? And what did he do for a job? (1 in 6). I recall so vividly leaving the baths in a dazed unfocused shock, everything echoing; a feeling of disassociation that has constantly revisited me until my recent recovery (a sensation that haunts for life as described by many CA survivors).

Whilst in a deep stretch on my back rack I was transported to the cloakroom next to the classroom where I had been taken after crying in the class, and I was sitting with the teacher Ms Skillan who was a bit scary. I could see her in my memory and for the first time she was speaking to me gently, encouraging me to say what was wrong but I wouldn't, couldn't speak. I was there, I was little Gregory, but I could observe and understand it all as I am now, an adult. Then my next memory came; I was home being grilled by the parents who were obviously very concerned, they'd received a letter, which one was holding, from the school asking them to go in and meet Ms Skillan and they were desperate to find out what was wrong. But their tone wasn't the same as hers because she was concerned for me whereas they were concerned for them, they were interrogating. When they returned 'the father' had obviously fallen out with Ms Skillan and didn't like her and got me to agree that she was horrid; I realized now she sensed there was abuse going on. The abuse stopped at home and I was treated differently, with even more suspicion. I became a reflection of their shame and guilt which the child will osmose and believe this is what they are, an embodiment of shame and guilt which in turn deadens self worth. This is a particularly insidious crippling effect of CA that haunts for a lifetime unless confronted.

For a few clear moments I was there: the dark cloakroom with one small window, Ms Skillan being so close and trying to coax me, I could even smell her. But I wouldn't speak out because I was conditioned to be silent by the parents. And next, the presence of the parents with this new energy I didn't recognize as a boy but now I did; their fear and their projection of blame onto me.

It was all there in my body. It had been held dormant for fifty years. In all that time I had never visited this memory, it had been locked away. It was another heavy slab of treachery, deceit and hopelessness I have come to be working through and deal with. Now I could physically extract it by moving it into my conscious mind and see it, hold and understand it, feel it and let it pass through. As a result my left shoulder, especially, has dropped and moves more easily.

The point I want to emphasize here is; I am way into recovery and thought nothing would come up from my body at this stage, but I was wrong. This was unexpected and uninvited, I wasn't looking for it but it came up.

As mentioned, I've suffered with 'a bad back' since I can remember. There's always been a knot slightly to one side of the top of my coccyx. It's been on going. This knot often grew in size and pain. Several times in my life I have been incapacitated, unable to walk, lying flat for days. Living with sciatic pain is no fun as those that do and have, will testify: a constant gnawing, stabbing pain depleting one's spirit. I never slept on my right side all my life.

After seeing specialists of various varieties over the years I submitted to accepting it has been, and always would be, a permanent condition.

The knot has now gone along with the forever dull throb and the phases of full on crippling pain. It has vanished like it never was there. It is like a miracle. Was it totally psychosomatic? In the past I had x-rays and there was speculation about a bulge in a disc, plus talk of a small scar on my back from an injury I can't remember (perhaps 'they' were looking for a pragmatic explanation?). I'd done some heavy duty yoga in the past – Hatha yoga style which is the 'bare knuckle variety' – stretching in one position for an age desperate to dig in to the knot, but it would return and I could never seem to get to its core. On a practical level I accepted my basic structure was damaged, but I noticed a correlation between my state of being and the pain, which I tried to track but could only say it was most acute when I wasn't feeling good about myself. I looked at this line of enquiry vaguely in the past but no one or nothing ever pointed me to the pain being psychosomatic, plus previously I looked to reject this concept because it might signal weakness of character and vulnerability which weren't allowed on my agenda.

Many trauma survivors choose, by way of protecting themselves against further abuse i.e. avoiding victim hood, to develop a tough shell, turning away from feelings of vulnerability. In parallel, as part of their sense of unworthiness, they often believe 'I am not allowed to indulge in any perceived weaknesses'. I upheld this camp of attitude.

After coughing blood into the bowl and further howling and convulsing whilst curled up on the floor of a public corridor, and considering the subsequent relief these incidents brought physically, spiritually, emotionally and mentally, I figured I would directly go for this knot in my back. I decided that it was psychosomatic and our relationship was over. Having made my mind up I knew I'd get rid of it and be able to do whatever it took with focused unrelenting determination, manage what ever came up and eject it from my body.

I recall as clearly as I might Christmas morning with my wonderful soul mate a short time ago but without the same feeling, being about six years old standing on the upstairs landing in the afternoon, probably a Saturday or Sunday and my sister's room was locked with her and Neville (the father) inside. There were odd noises and Vera (the mother) shooed me away and I asked what was happening.

'Daddy is teaching your sister how to be a woman,' was her response.

Ironically, Vera was a nursery school teacher but never talked to me when I was a little boy, or asked why I struggled to sleep, or why I wet the bed, or why I regularly vomited around my bed – (a reaction and defense mechanism).

A few weeks after they were both dead the house where they lived changed, the air inside became fresh and the colours brighter. The stench of evil had gone. Vera never listened to me ever. Even to the point of ignoring my directions if I knew where somewhere was when she was driving. My first therapist, who was well versed in dealing with troubled children, said 'she couldn't hear [me] because she didn't want to' – she didn't want to hear me cry out for help, she was trying to avoid her shame from not protecting me from the abuse the father was inflicting. But she interrogated my sister and I when we had been out and had interaction with others, especially grown ups, she needed to know every detail about what we had said. The guilt she carried had made her paranoid, as was the abuser. I understand many abusers are narcissistic and unable to take responsibility and therefore project blame for the abuse onto the victim thereby manifesting many psychological disorders, often self destructive. The survivor believes they are only worthy of abuse and become stuck, i.e. inviting from others and inflicting on the self, destructive patterns of behavior effectively reinforcing what the damage of the abuse has led us to believe about ourselves. We are comfortable with this cycle because we feel we are not worthy of anything better, and it is a pattern we are familiar with and therefore it is safe. The abuse survivor therefore reenlists abuse on themselves, for a lifetime. But this pattern is changeable. We can dig it out. We are worthy!

I dug into that small of my back. Dug and dug and dug. This was not like the previous unprompted convulsions. This was deliberate and unrelenting; trying every back stretch imaginable. Until at my Yoga class we did a 'pigeon', which for some reason I had never done – understand reader my forays into yoga have been in fits and starts with gaps of years – and whilst getting into it Donna suggested '...this one may bring up memories, and it may effect those who have endured trauma.' I became so tearful, flooded with a sense of guilt. I could feel Vera's voice questioning me with her angst, looking for me to have done or said something that may incriminate. I went back into the stretch at home in a controlled situation, plus other similar moves (in fact, going into more back bends than forward ones and especially, opening my hips – recognized as an area that hold emotions), and eventually the guilt and shame flooded out of the small of my back. I 'sat in the feelings'; a hot liquid filled my body, but not one that warmed me, it was acidic. I heard a thousand Vera's voices and felt this intense, abusive, fear loaded interrogation overwhelm me such that I wanted to bury myself in a hole on the beach like a little crab. But I squeezed and squeezed and went into it again and again. It has gone, so have the guilt and shame.

Another approach I got involved in was Cranial Therapy. By chance my yoga teacher had a friend studying a course and needed guinea pigs. Nicola seemed so young but she was an old soul full of wisdom with an instinct for healing. I did a little research into this practice but some things I choose to keep away from my intellect and leave as simply magical (like how a TV remote control works), which the whole experience was. CT certainly contributed to shaking free my back troubles. I recall after one session saying, 'wow I feel so free. I feel like I want to do the hula hoop!'

We talked about my childhood and she said something that stuck with me.

'The abuse is over. It is not the whole of you: it is now just a husk *you can be rid of.'*

Nicola was one of those people, those angels I mentioned that you will meet on your journey. They have gifts to help you on your way. Have faith, they are there waiting for you (ooo, I so love the label and concept of 'husk'…perfect…thank you Nicola).

I write all this by way of informing you how important bodywork has been for me. I give you examples of how trauma has been trapped in my body and how it has been removed. I wonder if at some point we will actually map the body and identify areas where trauma is held with the accompanying negative emotions. Like me, 'oh, pain in the small of your back, that's guilt.' That is not to say trauma held within the body is necessarily chartable. For example, it may be that imploded anger i.e. unexpressed anger is held in different ways by different people, although I suspect some generalities stick. The gut, particularly, holds negative stuff. My ulcer was imploded anger.

I recently got put onto TRE (Tension/Trauma Release Exercises). There is one move that sticks in my mind which I have since done several times. It involves lying on your back, legs bent and knees wide apart with the soles of your feet together, the outer edges on the floor. Push up with your hips and hold until you are about 80% knackered then put your feet together soles on the floor with your legs bent and knees together. Slowly part your knees and you may find, as I did/do, a point or points where you begin to shake. First time my body began shaking profusely and my gut pulsing, but the more I've done it the less pronounced the reaction has become. Notably, each time there weren't any accompanying emotions swamping the body, which is to be expected according to the teacher in the video I watched, therefore it is easy to handle; it just feels new and weird. The teacher suggested you may feel refreshed or tired; the latter for me, and I felt vulnerable and forlorn but this passed after a couple of days and plenty of rest. I've noticed I can handle more stress since, i.e. I don't get so irritable when things go wrong, as though my 'stress stack' got emptied out. I have always had a colon issue having had a duodenal ulcer caused by imploded stress and anger. Since my recovery the pain in my side had subsided considerably, but my recent adoption of TRE exercises have contributed to not having any pain at all in my lower left abdominal area.

TRE is an area I know little, but please see it as a lead I am offering you to look at and make a judgment as to whether it is a one you could pop into your kitbag! And when I say 'lead' may I suggest you properly check it out i.e. refer to qualified people.

Another tool, probably among others I haven't employed, is acupuncture. This got a mention the other day in relation to healing from childhood trauma. I tried it many years ago; I got pins stuck in my ears but I have to bow out here, I can't remember what for and what the result was, and I don't know anything about the subject either. Your on your own with this one – just an idea – might help.

One last one – tapping meridians....was mentioned recently. I have no idea what it means!.... (perhaps give Harry a call?)...Hey, we're brainstorming (bodystorming) here, new territory so all ideas are good ideas...!

Frankly, given a mandatory option of either reading about trauma or using bodywork, I would choose the latter i.e. action. That is to say over and above dealing with trauma on a cerebral level I would just work on the physical release, but that is me and again, it may not be for you. The right way is your way.

8. Reaching out & Declaration

I'm going to stick my neck out and say you're not going to recover from trauma on your own. I strongly suggest you enlist the help of others by telling them what you are going through and why you are going through it. This is reaching out. 'I need help!'

You may also be contemplating addressing the abuser – this is a separate issue.

Note: *I don't say 'your abuser' as this is more inclined to give you/me ownership of them and the abuse, and in that you may then choose to hold on to it more: be of a mindset engendering you to possess the abuse. 'My abuse'/ 'My abuser' have connotations of ownership: 'I've got this, this is mine.' The fault of the abuse lies entirely with the abuser. It is in the past. A large part of healing I have learnt and am still doing, is learning to 'let go' – using 'my', I think, does not help this. This is not my advice; I am passing on someone else's who has far more experience than I in decoding the effects of childhood abuse.*

Declaration of the abuse, the ensuing trauma and mental health difficulties I endured, is a subject I know a good deal about. I have told many people. I know plenty of people, including a large extended family, and I would be surprised if any of them don't know I had a nervous breakdown and I am a survivor of childhood sexual abuse. I now genuinely could not care less who knows it. In fact, the opposite, one major purpose of this book is to broadcast I am a survivor in order to enable others to speak out and shine a light on the effects of childhood abuse.

Declaration for me has definitely helped but to get to the point I am at takes many small steps. A non-swimmer wouldn't climb up the steps and dive off the high board straight off. They wouldn't want to and chances are they couldn't do it even if they got up the steps. And if they did dive they'd soon be in pain at best, and definitely not want to do it again. Declaration can be a bit like this: one step at a time. You need to build up your resilience.

Declaration is best done at your speed in your good time. No one can tell you when you should or shouldn't, and no one should. I'm just saying at least give it a go....but....there is definitely a big 'Aldo feet up' thing going on here. I need to get you into some armor to protect that 'courageous but vulnerable, beautiful creature that you are' (please feel free to keep repeating the last few words as many times as you like – substitute 'you are' with 'I am').

Reaching out comes before declaration. Reaching out is about asking for help because you are distressed (these definitions are mine - you may not agree with them). Declaration is telling people what you have endured, and particularly the why. I've split the two because you may at first, wisely in my opinion, choose to reach out for help by letting people know you are distressed but you don't want to share what has caused it.

Men don't reach out enough, hence the suicide rate (*single biggest killer of men under 45, the highest suicide rate is men 45-49, on average 12 men take their own lives everyday*). If my surrogate younger brother hadn't taken his life I would very possibly have killed myself. A wise man that knows about this stuff said to me 'vulnerability is strength'. I didn't get this at first. Going through life wearing a mask, making out everything is fine is foolish. It served you well up until this point but now you need to turn back into your pain and deal with it, and you are going to need help. It takes strength to turn around and let the mask drop and admit you are struggling. It takes strength to be vulnerable. It takes strength to fall back and allow humanity to catch you, it will, it caught me. You'd struggle to be more cynical about so called humanity than I was. But I had no choice, falling back and having faith in me and humanity was my only hope. I found it was the only hope I needed. It was there, now I see and feel it in abundance.

Here's the pragmatic Aldo bit: get your self care and self soothing plan in place first. Reaching out can prove to be bruising. Like I said, some people I expected to be there for me weren't. I reasoned I had invested so much time in listening and understanding them that I was in credit. Wrong. Perhaps, I didn't fit the role I played in their life anymore. It was possible they are survivors of trauma which they aren't accepting and processing, i.e. they go through life stuck in a holding pattern indirectly screaming for help by way of being a geyser of 'me talk': their own stack is full coping with life and they lack the emotional resource to be of much use. Some are not equipped to deal with people in an emotional crisis, they have no experience, and few have. This can leave you feeling bitter, reinforcing the idea you are alone and humanity is a sham. And there is grief in accepting the realization that some relationships you had aren't what you thought. But you need to conserve your personal resources and consequently the default, after all the cursing, vowing revenge, staring at empty hopelessness and feeling cheated, is to let them go. In hindsight, when you arrive at an objective viewpoint on your journey and take stock of your, most probably, rearranged relationships you'll be aware they are now based on *mutual* respect and care.

Another viewpoint is that you may be a people pleaser as survivors of CA often are. I probably was more than I would like to admit. We learn to create safety by being good to others, a survival technique used to appease the abusers. Perhaps also, over compensating for the abuse we endured by avoiding projecting any perceived abuse onto others. These default behavioral traits transcribe to the survivor's interactions whereby the agreement in a relationship becomes: 'it's all about the other person only'. The survivor feels unworthy of support and love from others; a neglectful childhood and/or childhood trauma can do this to you/me. Recovery includes breaking this agreement (you made it with you) and incorporating your needs into relationships i.e. by becoming more assertive and increasing self worth.

People can only do what they can do. They are not your abuser/s. Folk you think have failed you, forgive them, move on and create scope for other people waiting for you. To reprimand people you believe 'owe you support'? Why not just pop them in the bottom drawer for now because you may find they have another role in your life later on. *I recall Tom Hanks in 'Cast Away'; a man alone on a tropical island after a plane crash looking through the debris and finding a small white ice skate; hey just what he needed! But the blade turned out to be invaluable.*

In contrast, you must grasp this one: once you put you foot down towards the dark icy water, stepping stones will appear. People will appear in your life; people that understand, people that share, people that listen, you will love them and they will love you. And other people that are already in your life will transform right in front of you. You will see them differently. They may well have been on the periphery of your life but you will speak to them differently, more intimately; you will break through the usual code you shared. You will form much stronger bonds with some people already in your life.

Remember: right now you are wrong about stuff you think, and wrong about stuff you believe, but you don't know it, yet. What you are wrong about will reveal itself when you are ready. Eventually you will learn to want to be wrong, to embrace being wrong because it is there in this pain of realizing you are wrong that you find your growth and acceptance, thus your peace.

An inspiring close male survivor friend I met via 'group' went on to write a book about his life and recovery. He did a talk on a major radio channel and bravely, apart from going on the show, gave his email address. He received around four hundred responses from other survivors of child hood abuse and trauma to which he responded to all (his tenacity knows no bounds); two of them were from men (I understand that the audience was not typically female biased).

It is way, way beyond the act of the abuse itself. There are so many consequences that affect so deeply in such damaging ways. If people, everyone, could really understand this we would stop childhood abuse.

Publicly declaring I am survivor of CSA is therapeutic for me and hopefully it enables others to speak out about their troubles. Now I am at a stage whereby I can broadcast it out of, in part, a sense of duty and release, and by way of compensation for the massive journey I have been through.

But arriving at public declaration has taken a thousand steps.

Even after several therapy sessions when the subject of my childhood and CSA came up I was… 'what the hell has that got to do with you, or my situation now?...Back off…'.I did not, or want, to make the connection between my difficulties e.g. depression, with CSA. And that was with my therapist!

The first part of active recovery is acknowledging and speaking out about your distress. 'I feel depressed.' And further, should you choose, look at what may be fueling the distress. You may be able to identify you were traumatized as a child or as an adult, but you may not have been traumatized or may not be ready to make the connection, you are simply aware you are distressed, that's fine. Again, this is your journey.

I had made the decision to recover so I had to develop a strategy.

My first decision in terms of reaching out and declaration was to go against my natural instinct and share a lot. To speak out to many and keep reaching out. I accept that some may not be confident when speaking to others, in which case see the chapter on group therapy – a good start point. Once you've made the decision to keep pushing your self out there whilst accepting you may not always get the *ideal* responses then any lack of support or bad feedback won't hit so hard, you'll pick yourself up sooner rather than later and carry on. In short – reaching out is way better than not. In fact, I'll label 'reaching out' as a 'you definitely should'.

For those that respond in a less than ideal way, accept that they are not equipped to deal with your situation and drop the negative thinking about them, put them in a drawer and move on. They had a purpose in your life, they may well again. Some may bare the immediate brunt of your meltdown but others can't. Also, you may burn the first line of support out, it is unfair to keep dumping on the same people, and as you recover you can try not talking about your issues, it is not what life is all about. The 'drawer people' can get you back into 'normal' (for want of a better word) life, which I have been doing in the fairly recent past i.e. picking up with people I know would have been no use or weren't during my breakdown, but they can help me get back on the rails of life. It paid not to discount them forever. They weren't waterproof walking boots, they were sandals made for wearing at the beach cafe.

I operated on the basis the more people I told I was having a breakdown the more I help I would get. I was right. Just keep testing your boundaries i.e. coming out of your shell. The lure of hiding away all the time is a comfort and necessary at times; it is important to have safe 'you time' for rest and assimilation, but to grow and get stronger keep going back to the gym and lifting the weights, keep pushing yourself to lift more – get out of your comfort zone. To recover you have to take risks – go into the unknown and with that, let go of the known. Keep reaching out and sharing.

Why not? Fear. Fear of what? Ridicule, rejection, misunderstanding… You'll find the opposite happens. You will be embraced. By sharing my stuff I gained a wealth of insight as to what other people have gone through and are going through. You are not alone, you feel you are, but you are not. In the early stages of my breakdown I felt like everybody around me seemed to know what they were doing and what was happening: they appeared happy and robust. I was standing unnoticed at the side of a merry go round with all the brightly dressed happy people riding on wooden horses going round and round having a great time chatting and laughing, I was not involved and couldn't be, like little Gregory alone threading beads. Not so. There is a subtle tipping point when staying on your own hiding away will perpetuate the feeling of needing to be alone, and it becomes harder and harder to mix with others. Be mindful of this. No good sitting about waiting for the rescue squad. You are an adult now. You have to do this for you and importantly if abused as a child, the child within you. Give your child a voice. Heal your child.

'….yeah, you know what, I've been struggling recently, feeling depressed, then often really angst...'...a solid start…

Guess what? The other person you are talking to is a human and goes through the same emotions and thoughts as you (I struggled to grasp this one).

Declaration

This is about telling people more i.e. what caused your troubles.

I specifically separate this off from 'reaching out' because telling someone 'I am depressed' feels different to 'I am a survivor of childhood sexual abuse'. 'I am having difficulties sleeping because I am angst' vs. 'I am addicted to drugs and need them to sleep'.

But, the difference is more in your mind than the mind of the person you are telling. You feel the stigma more than they do.

I have read that if declaration is not for you then don't. For me it has been very cathartic.

On my art adventure I was actually selected from several hundred entries as one of twelve artists to be featured in an arts festival. I think it was because my 'bio' (bit of lingo) majored on me being a survivor of CSA and the healing of art. This 'Bio' was printed in the programme distributed and accessible to an unknown all. I actually played sax at the opening and, by coincidence, one of my pictures was centre stage so I'd unconsciously hijacked the whole event. I recall how I felt like I had climbed up to the high diving board as I gave the okay for my bio to be printed: that angst: that public declaration. A year later and a window of time between lockdowns, I picked up my pictures from an empty building and had to think and feel my way back to how I had been with that declaration, heading now rapidly towards wearing a sandwich board and shouting through a mega phone (and writing a book) about being a CSA survivor without a glimmer of doubt or angst. Now more resilient and robust, and further exhumed of the effects of trauma and more comfortable in my own skin for having spoken out and having received, at worst, only indifference, but largely support and understanding from all sorts of wonderful people. Trust me, fall back, people will catch you. I even got talking to two CSA survivors I'd never met at the opening gig of the art do!

You will be surprised where the support and understanding comes from. People will make themselves known to you. As you reach out and declare, they will greet you. And don't judge a book by its cover in terms of who is going to be the best help. I have a bunch of mates in London of full on 'geezers'. I had to laugh when one was telling me how he and another of the 'gang' were on a job, ('legit') just picking something up from a business, and the moment they walked in one of the employees took one look at them and immediately phoned the police! But I sat in front of them and sobbed some whilst telling them I was sexually abused as a child. Mockery? Revolt? Disdain? Rejection? Not a drip, only pure heartfelt support, and voice cracking whilst some shared of their own difficult childhoods of violent abuse and neglect.

Out of respect for myself I don't go around broadcasting out my journey and hurt as part of an introduction, it doesn't define me. If the topic of depression, addiction or other mental health difficulties arises I declare 'I've had my difficulties' which I associate with an 'abusive childhood'. Later, when I feel safe with the person, I will declare I was sexually abused as a child.

What are the chances of a negative response? I have told somewhere between sixty to eighty people, outside of groups etc, I was abused as a child and had only two negative responses – one from a lady who's catch phrase I later realized was '... well that's a laarrff [she was a bit posh] because...blah, blah'. I corrected her; it wasn't a 'laarrff' or a 'laff', far from it I levelly articulated. The other daft comment was from a doctor (GP) of all people, at the same practice I got help (but not the same doctor obvs), during a visit at the raw stage of my recovery about an unrelated physical issue. Again, I began to leak distress and told her what I was going through and why; she touched my arm and told me I should learn to forgive. I sobered up and found myself responding (in a similar fashion to Ms Laarrff) 'oh so you're a therapist too now?' She was way out of order: 1. giving 'should' advice and 2. 'forgiveness' is a massive topic and she was very wrong, I didn't have to. She was suitably jolted. Buuutttt….she was trying, and I did forgive her. She meant well.

NB there should be a common reaction by GP's to this declaration based on knowledge and understanding via education.

Know this: no one, but not one, of all the dozens of different people from all walks of life I have declared to have said anything disdainful.

I need to put in here an important note about declaring childhood abuse to members of your family where the abuser is a member of the family. I have done this, and spoken and shared with others that have. The results are a mixed bag.

Importantly, and I would label this a 'you should', is: declaring to family members about an abusive family member begs to be approached with planning and forethought. You may find it easier to share and declare with strangers, because you have no agreed social agenda.

Talking to family members about childhood abuse perpetrated by another family member needs pre-thought and planning otherwise the likelihood it will be bruising, and potentially damaging. I won't for the purposes of confidentiality identify specifically the reactions of members of my extended family since my realization and declaration of the abuse, but it has not always been good. When I say 'not always been good' the worst responses weren't overtly negative i.e. offensive or disparaging, but a minority either ignored me or were politely flat, like that of a customer service complaint department. In a phone call following a letter from me, one stated clearly they didn't want to hear anything about it – it sounded like a pre-rehearsed script, a post court case statement appended with 'no further comment', click, brrrrr. I took this to be cowardly and hopeless, and it added to my anger about the whole issue at the time. My therapist suggested their 'brittle response' pointed at something more, their own unresolved issues and those within the family..., hmmm, perhaps.

Of note is, I took the practical precaution of not, in the first instance, approaching them face to face as they may have reacted the wrong way [as I would see it] and consequently I may have reacted in the wrong way [to put it mildly]. I wrote to them i.e. handwritten posted letters (emails, by contrast, are recognized as the most misinterpreted form of communication), and then spoke to them on the phone or tried to.

Two points I need to make here. The reactions may not be positive; some won't be I would bet. Try as you might you *will* create ideal responses in your mind in advance, and in my own experience, echoed by other survivors, the absolute ideal may not be met, in fact the odds are against it. And I stress, you will most likely hope their responses will be healing, that their reaction will go along way to giving recompense for the abuse, but please beware, there is a possibility of a big disappointment. Plus, you will be hyper sensitive to any feedback on this subject which means so much to you and, as such, even a flat response will be perceived by you as a huge negative.

If you are declaring about childhood abuse, and I think particularly if it is sexual abuse, you can expect some to recoil from this news. If it has happened within their family they probably don't want to be tarred by this brush; they may have the perception it is a reflection on them in some way and will protect themselves from the news by rejecting you. They may feel guilt for not having stopped it and thus it may become about them rather than your pain. They will most probably have a perception of CSA they don't want to entertain in their minds, and may have an idealized view of the abuser and do not want to sully it: they want things to be nice in their World. And remember, you have prepared, they have not.

Yes, it is you that are the victim of the abuse. You deserve the compensation of love and support. But they are entitled to their opinion, view and reaction. The truth is: you will probably not figure out what they are thinking, you have to accept this and not get stuck, you must let go – they are not your abusers. I truly get this is far from easy to do. And whilst they may recoil in the first instance, they may change their outlook in time and, by the same token, your feelings towards their response will be different a year from now. For me, I simply decided not to invest any emotional energy in the family members who weren't supportive as with those I thought were close friends, as for the former I simply lost respect for them and the latter I just don't expect anything of them, and wouldn't especially help them. There is grief with this. There is grief with all change; grief with letting go of a belief.

Forgive them for they know not what they do.

In contrast, I got three wonderfully supportive reactions from two cousins and an aunty. I take the positives and leave the rest behind. Those positives especially, were more fuel for my recovery. One way or another I personally had to get through the declaration process, otherwise for me it [declaring to my family] would always have sat there looking at me…should I or shouldn't I… 'what will they do and say and think?'…well, that stone has been lifted and looked under and dealt with, as such I can move on. And for sure, the positives outweigh the negatives. Well, I don't hold the negatives so there is nothing to weigh, my net gain is the gold left in the pan.

But I add: it is documented that declaration of abuse within a family is more often divisive than not. I know of five men that have experienced familial abuse and have declared as such to other family members and all report it to be divisive, but in balance are glad they did.

Declaring directly to your abusers?

I have only communicated with people that have, and again a mixed bag in terms of the immediate response. Typically i.e. it is documented, abusers will deny and stick to denial. This can be re-traumatising.

I will back off a bit on this subject but will say this: get into a strong place, a good way down the road of recovery, and get help lined up, preferably professional help and support; even be accompanied by a professional. And prepare as much as possible, spiritually, emotionally, physically, and psychologically, and arm yourself with a planned dialogue/script (to an extent at least – this gives you rails to go along in the heat of the encounter). Importantly, have set plan about what you are going to do afterwards that is all about nurturing you, no matter how tough you think you are. Be the best you can be for yourself.

Encountering the abuser is a big one. Think it through.

But know this: you don't have to do it. It isn't necessary for recovery. And know that if you do, it's done, you did it; you process it and move on. You may have wanted the abuser to beg your forgiveness and they didn't, but now you know. You did it because you needed to do it. Or, you didn't do it because you didn't need to. Both ways are right. And if you are not sure, then certainly it is a process that needs discussion with allies, and you can decide not to decide i.e. shelve it and go back to the idea later.

9. 'You Stuff' (expression & creativity)...play

Let's lighten up for a bit (it's allowed).

I've decided to bundle this lot together. They are about self expression. They are part of the self care programme. All of the survivors I know are into creative activity to the point they talk about them with possessed passion. Play offers a parallel to, and escape from, what can be the toil of the recovery process and relief from the often debilitating effects of trauma which can make life into a serious endeavor, making you feel you are not allowed to have pleasure along the way. You may feel unworthy and play feels incongruent. This is far from the case.

Recall activities you once enjoyed but haven't done for an age, or stuff you have considered but never got round to. You now have good reason. You are recovering from trauma. Doing stuff that aids expression of you is of enormous benefit on many levels; meditative, increasing sense of self worth, belonging, release: all very therapeutic. It nourishes the soul.

A day I don't indulge in creativity is a day wasted. I got into painting as a therapeutic vehicle. When I paint I think of little else. We need 'to get out of ourselves in a healthy way. Also, painting was something I loved when I was a little boy. I channel my inner child when I am painting which is healing, and when I've done each picture the process is done, I don't do it for the approval of others. There is a process here I went through additional to the other benefits; it became my vehicle to getting past the need for the approval of others, living to be a people pleaser which childhood abuse survivors often are (as mentioned). It may be we had to devise ways of being unobtrusive, hiding our feelings, not being difficult, be pleasing to our abusers so as to survive. It may be we endured a lack of emotional support; enduring neglect therefore always seeking the approval of others, always calling for their support which is carried through to adulthood: always sacrificing oneself in order to feel we are pleasing others therefore trapped in the role of victim. Painting was one escape from this trap, guiding me to consciously recognize that not everyone, in fact few, would stop and look at my work and say 'that's really good'. I got plain fed up with the feeling of being at their mercy, waiting for their opinion. I recognized within me what was going on. I grasped the idea that others are entitled to their judgment which is as valid as mine (errr…okay I'm stretching it a bit now), that we and our tastes are all different (a great thing), and 'Greg, just get over yourself' – a therapist would never say this, they just can't (code/Omerta – but some elements you've just got to push past and move on). I even stopped asking people what they thought. I consciously recognized I was painting for me. This need to seek approval and people please at my cost became significantly reduced. I cite painting to explain a change of thought process and way of being.

Partake in new and old pursuits as part of your recovery. You will learn lessons serving to compliment and aid your recovery. Activities will take on a greater meaning; you will receive them in a deeper dimension, beyond recreational, mark my words.

I no longer frown at the ground; I turn slowly, infused with awe at the forest.

Busking was another process that helped with this. I regularly busk to this day. There is a wonderful defiant freedom in it plus a sense of being part of and giving to the community. I busk with a friend. People give money I perceive as tokens, gestures of *gratitude*. We certainly don't do it for the financial reward as it doesn't pay well at all. But there are so often moments of pure spontaneous joy and a fierce connection with humanity, although the positives can be balanced against a feeling of gloom as people file by ignoring us. I sometimes feel so vulnerable performing, spiritually exposed. But I busk first and foremost for me. I do it because I enjoy playing. Plus, before I play I create an *intention*. I've decided in advance what I am going to concentrate on. What part of my playing am I going to work on; my breathing, the high notes, holding a note, rhythm, or decide to just let go, and I review with myself afterwards. What did I gain by way of my own investment in me? And I recognize and acknowledge the gain. This way I don't need the approval of others. If we get good feedback, and we often do because we can both play, then great, even better.
Go into 'you stuff' with *intention*: 'I am doing this for me'. As with your recovery: go in with *intention*. Plus, you are doing the hard work for you, not foremost the approval of others: this way your recovery will stay on steadfast rails.

Writing about your abuse and recovery is widely recognized as a very therapeutic investment of your time in you, and one reason I am writing this book; helping me consolidate my thinking and giving me a path to go along. Akin to journaling your Odyssey of recovery, it gives you a *voice*. Your trauma may well have been caused in circumstances that were shrouded in secrecy, so writing about it and your recovery helps you express it, step away and view it which helps expulse the effects of the trauma.

Several sources recommend journaling one's journey of recovery because writing creates clarity from confusion and helps shed negatives. When I look back at my 12 steps notes I don't relate to several answers, I recognize the hand writing but have to make a conscious mental effort to grasp the points I made regarding my attitudes, the way I was thinking and feeling. Remember it was totally confidential, totally authentic: there was nothing external influencing my words. It is useful to look back and be able to actualize the change, the progress.

Maintaining a journal measures how far you have traveled, important to acknowledge. It is easy to think you are getting no where, to believe the future is devoid of hope. Not so. Read the journal. You've changed. Life is becoming easier. I read my responses to the twelve steps questions and think 'wow, fancy going through life thinking that...' some of my thoughts are alien now. Similarly, some responses remained the same each time I passed through which I accepted until I wondered if I was stuck on these issues and therefore may benefit from another view. In essence, the questions with the same answers held the key to the most movement for me, the most challenge. Why am I holding tightly to a viewpoint?

'I can't draw.'
Or perhaps... 'I'm afraid of being vulnerable: exposing myself to criticism and lack of approval from others.'

As part of my quest to become a professional artist (life plan no. mmcxxxviii) i.e. do more than give away pictures to friends at my insistence, I was hawking my wares around an exhibition centre in London filled with stands representing art galleries (there are dozens and dozens – beyond the big ones we all know about) who were in turn hawking their wares to the visitors i.e. potential buyers of art (paintings mostly).

Implementation of plan B (of above life plan) was to approach stands at the exhibition rented by galleries displaying art looking a bit like mine. *Plan A involved phoning galleries up trying to flog my stuff, and on one occasion I recall a chap with a posh voice asking if I'd seen their web site. 'I hadn't' I confessed. I was calling dozens and didn't have time to wade through a load of web sites first; just go through the numbers I figured, but I didn't tell him this. 'Thought not,' he said, and suggested it might've been a good idea. 'Why' I asked. 'Because,' he said, 'our artists all have something in common.' 'What's that?' I enquired. 'They are all dead,' said he*. So 'plan B', which subsequently involved a modicum of qualification, was in action.

Point is: I spotted a very well heeled mature couple staring at a piece of 'art'. I had already looked at it. It was a piece of lined A4 paper, the type you might find in any stationers anywhere. On it was scribble done in pencil. A five year old, neigh, a two year old could have done it, and if by a two year old I would have appreciated it because my favorite art is by people under the age of twelve, it is unaffected. This was the opposite; it was just silly (in my opinion). It was, however, in a nice frame and priced at a mere twenty five thousand pounds, but wasn't by an artist that would typically be a household name. I approached the couple and politely, so that they would be open with me, asked a couple of questions. It transpires they knew of the artist and 'liked to see the formation of thought', and were truly thinking of buying it.

1. Art is subjective.

2. You can draw. You can do anything.
3. What have you got to lose? Potentially £25 g's to gain (who's going to mock you then?)
4. …so, whatever it is, give it a go…

I am not suggesting you must get into art, just don't hide behind the 'I can't do that, I'm no good at it' excuse. And doing something new, a challenge, will help you in your recovery. It teaches you to be vulnerable, accept new things, get out of the comfort zone, and gives healthy distraction. Distraction can be a holiday for the mind and soul. You are going into a change period. Paralleling this period with a new or revisited activity you enjoy is a big help. Do it for you.

All the people I know from groups who moved a good way on the recovery journey have taken up new hobbies; started doing something they've always wanted to do, they're even making a living and/or a lifestyle, out of a new way of life. One survivor lady I know is now a semi pro boxer, never boxed before her recovery journey.

I've mentioned the busking; I read somewhere that along with another language learning an instrument is good for the brain. In that, a chap was telling me about the resonance of certain music. It's widely accepted music has a profound effect on us. It's no secret certain music will serve to calm you. On that note, it can be easy to forget: forget to separate time out and listen to some calming music. There is evidence proposing musical vibration resonates with us and affects our mood. I don't know much about the technicalities. Just a reminder that's all, (ahup, time for me gong bath!)

I was deliberately listening to Samuel Barber: Adagio for Strings when I wrote this last paragraph. I fully appreciated it when a survivor brother shared a link to a radio interview given by a successful rugby player who talked in a heart wrenching way about how he was abused as a child and the effects into adulthood, and then, by his choice, they played this piece.

For me, I need projects running alongside my life only involving me; activities without the need for anyone else, except their absence: for me, it, the thing/hobby etc, requires its own journey. Not something I just do, I need to feel it leads somewhere, provides its own route of exploration. When I 'practice' on my saxophone once finished it's gone, no body heard, it wasn't recorded, it was purely for me. But each time I feel like I am building, moving forward, discovering. It doesn't matter that my input is not externally measurable or recognized. The point I am trying to make is: the 'do' will provide collateral you can use as a stepping stone by way of taking you out of yourself on this intense journey. It will form a rock, an anchor, an escape, a parallel, a companion, and a sensation of movement.

It is said survivors have an instinct about their journey and how it should unfold when, how, and at what pace. You are on a long journey, an Odyssey, so allow yourself break periods.

To not recover whilst recovering i.e. to make resting from recovery and doing positive alternatives is vital, otherwise you condition yourself into always and only 'being in recovery' and/or 'healing', subsequently choosing to be defined by the trauma. In my opinion, actively seeking to perpetuate a permanence of 'healing from trauma' becomes a safety, an excuse not to let go and live which has a hefty price tag i.e. the loss of living beyond oneself with engaged courageous passion, or just simply having a ‘laff’ or a ‘laarff’ even.

Part C – Big Topics

1. Addiction

A massive topic.

Following are two articles I wrote, one was published in a booklet procured by a charity called One in Four titled 'Numbing the Pain', a collection of stories by ex-addicts and CSA survivors, circulated to GP's around the UK I believe. The latter was published in British Association for Counselling & Psychotherapy magazine (& website – with podcast) 'Therapy Today' circulated to all its members.

Lying in bed aged seven I wouldn't know what time but the traffic had been quiet for a long while. I would be wide awake staring at the gap of the door, my heart pounding, paralysed by fear, waiting for the bogey man……….some forty years later I caught myself lying on the kitchen floor at maybe three o clock in the morning on a week night. I was trying to lift the washing machine with one hand whilst looking and scraping underneath with a bit of fashioned cardboard. I was sure some drugs had fallen there.

Everything should have been fine but I was constantly tearful. 'Don't cry or I'll give you something to cry about' was the father's mantra. Now middle aged I hadn't cried since I couldn't remember. Emotions were for others, the weak if I'm honest: they weren't allowed. I've since learnt that stopping the child from expressing their feelings helps protect the abuser, keeps them cloaked. Suppression of my feelings was engrained.

I'd accepted that I had a compulsive, addictive personality. It was a curse, my cross to bear, just the way I was made.

I had dragged it around all my adult life. If it wasn't alcohol it was drugs or gambling, or all. I had learnt to hide and deny. It was under control according to my delusion. But there would be periods when I wouldn't function and I'd fall into the abyss. The voice of my addiction could change and adapt so as to speak to me, the best way, the direct way, the subtle and powerful way, but always a constant in my life, my loyal companion.

I'd hit a wall. I wasn't joining in with life anymore and was constantly tearful. I was back to sitting inside quietly threading beads when the other children were out playing in the sun. No matter which way I looked forward there wasn't a way through. The World was doom; life was hopelessness but my companion was there, my companion who took its' toll. It took my integrity. It chipped away at it. The sacrifice of my integrity took with it my conscience, my real connection to others, and so it took my soul. I didn't know that and I didn't want to, I didn't want to hear it. I had to numb at any cost.

The white hot cauldron of hate, of anger, of resent, of self-loathing: the darkness of doom, angst, despair and hopelessness would rise up and overwhelm me, a suffocating python. I had to escape being me. But I had my companion, my addiction.

Now I'd hit a wall. I was constantly tearful. I was leaking. My companion wasn't working anymore. A close friend had hung himself: this was his choice and an option I had wrestled with many times, an out which was okay with me. Seeing the pain it caused I figured I'd try and carry on no matter how hard the python squeezed. Then an older cousin died and I grieved so much. I grieved and grieved too much: more than I could understand, and I couldn't numb out anymore.

I felt a new inner voice trying to speak to me.

The sun was shining through the blinds in my flat. I adjusted them and the sound and the light cast me back to my twenties when I went to stay with that cousin who had settled in Australia. They had the same blinds. Then it made sense. I had a moment beyond a clear thought, more a halting realisation. When I was a small boy my older cousin who grew big quick, used to stay with us at Christmas and sleep in my room. It was the only time I felt safe. Safe from the bogey man. Safe from the father: the abuser. My cousin's death took away what little sense of safety my inner child had.

From an early age I was abused by the father I had. And I was also abused by a man at the swimming baths. The abuse stained my soul with confusion and fear. I was alone.

The abused child is traumatised and cannot process, speak out, understand, prevent. The child is suppressed and manipulated and becomes an object of shame, a feeling which possesses them all their life. The World is no longer wondrous. It is only a World of fear from which the child has no escape. The child can only suppress the fear and shame and guilt they feel, and bravely carry on in this hopeless frightening World because they have no choice or voice. The child learns to survive. Learns to numb.

Childhood abuse is an international epidemic. As many as one in four females and one in six males suffer childhood sexual abuse. Consider the scale of this. We are now recognising its existence. Not just recognising, but realising its magnitude and the harm it causes. An abused child is damaged for life from the moment it happens unless dealt with. The harm can create addiction. The need to numb. The need to escape that caldron of feelings that bear so heavy. Addiction is part of the survival. It is the companion that many survivors like me need.

We have shone a bright light on childhood abuse. We need to talk and talk about it. We see it as a darkness in society that we previously ignored: we turned our backs on it and let the survivors suffer in silence. But no more. That light must get brighter. We must understand the effects of abuse on the child and the effects throughout their lives. Together we will find the ways to stop Childhood abuse.

The survivors? Those courageous people who live in continual torment. Those that have found a way through. We become overwhelmed with despair, with doom, possessed with anger, self-loathing, shame and guilt, believing the abuse was in some way our fault, and so often we become addicts. We live a half-life because a full life without the companion of addiction is too much to bear.

I'd hit a wall. The old behaviour pattern of numbing stopped working and there felt like no way forward anymore, only total self-destruction.

That new voice was mine. My child within. It was time to listen to him and feel what he felt. So began my Odyssey to recovery......

If what I have said talks to you then I will tell you clearly: you have made it this far and so proved you have the strength and courage to take that journey. You owe it to your inner child. That child who survived.

The python weakens. It let's go. The voice of your addiction fades. You get to choose, no longer compelled to numb.

Reach out. Say what happened to you. You are not alone. People will listen and believe you. You will realise that you are a survivor. You are a warrior. You have an undefeatable indefatigable spirit.

Light will come into your life and you will feel peace.

You will love yourself because you are beautiful. A beautiful pure soul lives within you.

It's time to rescue your child. Go through the journey. Feel and feel and feel until you are totally exhausted and feel more and the light and peace will come my friend. I know, I have seen it, I have felt it.

Self love and joy of life will possess you

Conversations with Carl – Addiction & Therapy – (published in Therapy Today – February '21 issue)

Walking the Thames towpath I caught up with a man I assessed, given that I was hyper vigilant, to be bigger and stronger than me. When he glanced back I sensed he was also hyper vigilant and I intuited a survivor too.

'If I sneaked up on you I'd wear a different jacket', rustling as I walked. We chatted and walked together from then on most days until he left London. We shared that we were marijuana addicts. He'd stopped via an intensive 12-steps programme. I had returned transitorily to 'dope' at that time, and we shared about our abusive childhoods.

He conquered his addiction via pure will power. Me eventually via, in large part, therapy albeit indirectly i.e. as a by-product of recovery from the effects of trauma caused by Childhood Sexual Abuse.
Addiction, I believe, is escape. Escape to a 'safer' place. Escape from being with the thoughts and feelings that are

overwhelming: too hard to be with. Addiction is perceived as a safe exit. You think you choose it, but eventually it chooses you.

There is an argument, evidenced by Carl's success, for the 'military' approach to conquering addiction i.e. after recognition, acceptance, and adherence to a programme with accompanying peer support. Tackling addiction head on requires pure will power: conscious abstinence. Without consistent will power forcing the establishment of new habits, new neural paths, addiction will return. The wound will re-open, fester and addiction will manifest.

So, why is the addiction there?

Cut out the addiction or cut out the cause?

Cutting out the cause requires therapy, and for me addiction eventually drifted away. Put simply, I didn't approach my addictive behavior directly in therapy. Through therapy I became aware I used marijuana to numb feelings of intense anger or hopelessness, that my addiction to gambling was to create escapism via excitement and to re-expose myself, ultimately, to shame. Through therapy I dealt with the underlying issues, the root of all being the trauma of CSA.

If you don't know that abuse in childhood inflicts trauma that generates crippling emotional and mental health issues which last, if unresolved, a lifetime: then as a health professional you need to catch up.

Therapy was a combination of digging deep: being with the trauma that CSA caused and understanding cerebrally the effects; accepting the construct of a family that is perpetuating and hiding abuse by disabling the child's (my) emotions; learning to be with and dissipate intense anger, shame, guilt, lack of trust and self worth. Understanding and choosing to work on my need to generate safety through a complex array of behaviors that were often destructive and no longer served me, an endless jungle of other intertwined stuff deeply rooted and all embalmed with addictive behavior. Addiction was my antidote; I swapped it for therapy, group therapy, body work, conscious behavioral choice, self care, et al.

From aged seventeen to my breakdown at fifty three I always had marijuana in my life. Oh the relief of the first smoke, I was forever trying to get back to it. It became my constant companion through life.

Events including deaths, inability to get work, loss of purpose and the suffocating sense of doom always haunting me became stronger and I weaker. The constant belief that it was not 'if' but 'when' I would kill myself came into sharp focus. But my surrogate younger brother had committed suicide and the proceeding devastation caused me to vow not to, so after a GP in Gloucester claimed I wasn't depressed I stepped up the addiction, chain smoking three joints first thing in the morning.

Moving to London by way of gathering hope I managed to drop the drugs for two years, a stretch for me. Visiting the GP there with an arm problem on leaving I broke down and sobbed and she asked if I wanted to 'talk to someone'. I conceded that I needed to. For a year an experienced lady changing her modality joined what became my Odyssey of recovery.

I saw another therapist for a year after that. Different styles - dictated more by the therapist than the method I say. I decided to choose the positives in order to recover.

Now I am free. Addiction parallels an afternoon spent recently staring at a photo on-line I'd never seen: a school photo when I was fourteen. I couldn't truly define what I, that boy, was thinking and feeling. There was grief in that, like the passing of my acquaintance the addiction. But change happens, it is possible. I am no longer that fourteen year old boy and similarly, I am no longer an addict. I have moved on.

A number of Adverse Childhood Experience (ACE) studies have found that ACE's such as physical, emotional and sexual abuse increase the risk of addiction (Felitti et al 1998). Individuals who have experienced more than four ACEs are seven times more likely to be addicted to alcohol, ten times more likely to be at the risk of intravenous drug addiction and twelve times more likely to have attempted suicide.

1 in 4 females and 1 in 6 males experience childhood sexual abuse.

- A 2005 study conducted by the U.S. Centers for Disease control, on San Diego Kaiser Permanente HMO members, reported that 16% of males were sexually abused by the age of 18.

- A 2003 national study of U.S. adults reported that 14.2% of men were sexually abused before the age of 18.

- A 1998 study reviewing research on male childhood sexual abuse concluded that the problems is "common, under-reported, under-recognized, and under-treated."

- A 1996 study of male university students in the Boston area reported that 18% of men were sexually abused before the age of 16.

- A 1990 national study of U.S. adults reported that 16% of men were sexually abused before the age of 18.

Why these statistics are probably underestimates:

- Males who have such experiences are less likely to disclose them than are females.

- Only 16% of men with documented histories of sexual abuse (by social service agencies, which means it was very serious) considered themselves to have been sexually abused, compared to 64% of women with documented histories in the same study.

Men who've had such experiences are at much greater risk than those who haven't for serious mental health problems, including:

- Symptoms of post-traumatic stress disorder and depression.

- Alcoholism and drug abuse.

- Suicidal thoughts and suicide attempts.

- Problems in intimate relationships.

- Underachievement at school and at work.

****

Acknowledging you are an addict is the first step. Understanding why you are an addict is a journey, as is decoding what to do about it. So there is declaration to yourself which is entirely up to you, and has to come from you otherwise you will never accept your condition and therefore you won't get past first base.

'Hello my name is Greg and I am an addict.'

I visited 'the father' some years ago. He was drunk at 4pm, fell and bounced off the edge of the bed onto the floor. I told him he was an alcoholic and he sternly replied whilst looking up at me 'I am not an owlcohowic.' I stepped over him and said 'I think that is called irony.'

Enter stage left, brutal self honesty.

Years later my wife found me lying on the floor lifting up the washing machine and looking under it for some dope that had fallen behind it.

'You are an addict just like your father,' she said. That hurt. He was long since dead but the thought of being associated with him: not good. The idea I was an addict grew until I accepted it. I actually thought everyone would go around stoned all day if they could. I had to declare to myself that I was an addict.

I started a period of intense depression around that time to the point where my wife would look me in the eye before she left for work, (I wasn't contributing to society), and make me promise I would be alive when she got back: that I wouldn't commit suicide. Firstly, I had to admit to myself I was chronically depressed. Everything was closing in; being permanently stoned was the only antidote other than suicide. But this time it wasn't working.

We moved towns in search of new hope and a change of personnel for me i.e. dealers. I managed to take a good long break from my addiction and with that my volcano of blocked emotions was unplugged.

After the first stage of my breakdown, which began in October 2015, I took to contributing by doing volunteer work at homeless centers, as mentioned. Remember the therapist at one centre who previously worked exclusively with addicts but gave up? She found it a thankless and hopeless exercise. The successes were so few it corroded her spirit.

I totally get why that was so. Her experience points at the reality: escaping from, conquering, quitting, leaving behind, letting go of addiction is very, very hard.

Those that are not or haven't been addicts, never truly understand.

Addiction: defined (for our purposes) as being anything having medium or long term negative effects on one's life but the person keeps doing it anyway.

In order to stop change the now.

We can therefore be addicted to anything. Some things have a considerable negative effect.

My go to addiction, as declared, was marijuana. I totally loved the stuff for years and then finally I grew to be suspicious of it, realizing it was responsible for dozens of really awful destructive decisions in my life in a multitude of ways, and destructive to those around me, not forgetting my health. Then I despised it, knowing it owned me: then I became totally reliant on it to get me from day to day, every day.

You are advised to get help if you are going to beat addiction. Addiction weaves itself into the very fabric of your being. It becomes your life support system. Rather like 'Alien' where the 'thing' connects with you and in time the victim becomes wholly reliant for survival on the 'thing'. Trouble is we won't admit it. We won't recognize we are addicts. The being an addict, we think, carries stigma. It feels like admitting a terrible weakness: admitting a personal immorality. That being an addict is being a leper in society. It is incredible the lengths we go to avoid self truths. I heard (read perhaps) we all live in a deluded state to an extent. *It could be argued that having hope, which is part of our survival, is to be in a deluded state. I used to believe to be hopeful is to be delusional. Now I don't.* The point is: we become, I became, deluded about my addiction. I was not, in my reality, an addict. I never considered this concept. I simply went around stoned all the time always knowing how much dope I had and several dealers' numbers on my phone. Always knew no matter what I was or wasn't doing that within a known amount of time I would be rolling a very strong joint which became skunk weed only, always steadily increasing the dose. I reckoned if other people had the where with all to go around stoned all the time they would, somehow they were fools and I had it figured out. More fool them for putting up with this life of despair! I had dope, hooray for me. Except I was having coughing fits, and was wasting good money and was waiting around in awkward circumstances for people that couldn't tell the time whilst compromising my integrity and making streams of crap decisions and alienating people and thinking I was integrating but they were humoring me and I stunk and was talking nonsense and not achieving anything whatsoever and only having 'friendships' with addicts and dealers and not truly engaging with my wife or my life or anything and when I paused because a dealer let me down I would get downright edgy and nasty and irritable and caustic and feel violent and hopeless and depressed and destructive and I would implode. And then back round and round the garden, but not like a pleasant teddy bear, more like a sad fool; sad because I didn't know it. I didn't know the cycle I was in or, moreover, I didn't see another way beyond the cycle.

Admitting addiction is a big thing. It felt like a self betrayal: like admitting defeat. Like everything I have amounted to, everything I have done, even all the positive things, amount to nothing: that my life was an empty shell: that I was empty shell: then finally the realization that addiction wasn't the answer; it wasn't the icing on the cake.

It's said the addict has to hit their own low point. The low point of epiphany when they finally see themselves for what they have become, initiating the decision to do something – commit to doing something about it: the catalytic low point I call it.

I had my own low point. It is personal to me. I almost don't want to share because that may expel the shame the memory creates which I need to preserve by way of a fall back motivator i.e. I don't ever want to get that low again (shame does have a positive purpose). I speak without qualification for all ex-addicts when I say it is a revelation to oneself how many low points one can go down to and through, before getting to the one that does the trick. *(Lying on the floor lifting up the washing machine became quite passé and an ineffective gauge of my decline during that period – the catalytic low point was discovered several fathoms below and I had what I can only describe as an outer body experience when I saw myself, possibly like the time, I've heard it said, when one has just died; when you float above your body and truly see yourself for the first and only time. An amalgam of my spirit at all ages at all times in my life floated above me and observed and judged deservedly: my treachery of me).*

We moved towns by way of starting afresh after the low point. I decided not to buy any weed and to stop gambling. Keep it simple. I got out and did stuff. I busked, but before I went out each morning I began to cry, it just kind of leaked out. Now I was clean my inner child and the pain I/he had been holding back was coming through. I'd numbed it out long enough. The giant elastic band I'd pulled on all my life was now stretched to its limit and I could pull no more, and then I had that arm problem and went to see my doctor.

I haven't studied the science but I'm aware there's talk of addictive personality traits being inherited, an addictive gene almost. I understand it is imprecise i.e. it is not, I understand, a given that one inherits addictive behavior purely because of genetics. For what it is worth, I would say that becoming an addict is to an extent inherited, one is predisposed to becoming an addict via genetics, but being a witness to addictive behavior during childhood and subsequent trauma plays a much stronger role. More nurture than nature in my opinion. I don't subscribe to the 'addiction is totally inherited and there is nothing, or a limited amount you can do about it' script, which I view as an excuse. Addiction is curable. And note: there is a difference between stoppable and curable. To become an ex-addict, in my opinion, you must do both. You can't be cured if you don't stop, and you can't stop permanently if you're not cured, or at least it will make the rest of your journey more about abstinence rather than being cured i.e. consciously not doing the behavior, as opposed to not needing to.

Addiction is a safety. Addiction is an escape. It is an escape from facing into the 'what is'. Not facing the 'what is' is driven by the fear of the feelings the 'what is' creates. Addiction is therefore about turning away from one's own feelings that threaten to overwhelm. It is a safety blanket, a favorite teddy.

You may be an addict, an ex-addict, or someone that has dealings with addicts, and may have strong opinions on this subject. I am giving mine, my opinions and how I view it, but as I write it feels right.

I was interviewed the other day for BACP podcast and the interviewer raised the point that some therapists won't see a client who is an addict. Isn't it 'chicken and egg'? How does one stop the addiction first in order to get to the cause, rather than resolving the cause in order to stop the addiction? Where do you start? My answer: one has to stop the addictive behavior first. This is not to say that the person is cured of the addiction. They have simply stopped the behavior.

The straightforward way is to 'cold turkey' which is tough and you will probably need support. Here the twelve steps are useful if there's a discipline related to your addiction. I stopped the dope and within months I began leaking emotions; these were familiar feelings signaling the onslaught of depression which, indirectly, prompted the engagement of therapy and within a handful of sessions the dam broke and a Tsunami of feelings hit and my breakdown came. I had gone through the 'cold turkey' bit, the immediate often minute by minute doing battle with the urge to smoke dope to the point where the compelling urges had died right down, I had chopped the branches, but it was the therapy, in large part, that helped me dig out the roots, or at least identify and understand the roots.

During the podcast I was given the update that some therapists won't see addicts. The question that came to my mind after the podcast was...

A man goes to see a therapist and says, 'I need help. I'm a drug addict.'

'You must get clear before I'll see you,' responds the therapist.

'Why?' says the man.

'Because you are using drugs to numb out from the overwhelming feelings and you will not process fully the work you need to do because you will be in an altered state. Plus, the process of therapy will have a profound effect and may push you further into taking drugs.'

Six months later....

The man says -

'I need help. I am clear of drugs. Now I take psychotropic medication'.

(Or rather, 'I need help. I've swapped numbing out on illegal drugs for legal drugs.')....

...addicts may well need professional help to wean them off the habit with a view to navigating to, and beyond, the cause/s. A vital bridge on the journey to recovery denied by 'the profession' (e.g. NHS, I am informed by a distressed mother of an addict)...leaving the abandoned addict with the solace of...?

A book I read by a chap that knows the terrain of being a male survivor of CSA stated it is far from unusual for survivors of CSA (and I add all childhood abuse) to become addicts because of the need to numb out. Survivors who are addicts add conquering addiction to the list of immensely difficult processes they must go through in order to recover, as if it were *only* a further burden. Yes, but I also see my relationship with my ex-addiction as a barometer of where I am at in terms of my recovery from CSA. Having conquered addiction makes me feel indestructible.

Let me be clear, and it is important to have a picture painted of the (your) potential future, I don't smoke dope anymore. I live in London and each time I go out nine times out of ten I will smell that distinctive aroma of marijuana. People smoke it in public around here. I used to be able to, and probably still could, get dope anywhere in the World because I've been all over the World and I've smoked dope everywhere I've been. Getting dope in our area is easy but now I don't consciously abstain from buying it or especially avoid it and say 'no' to myself for any of a multitude of reasons e.g. 'I'll be letting myself down, destroying all the hard work I've done, letting other people down, feel guilty and be disgusted with myself afterwards…' etc, neither do I have a regime in my mind evangelizing about the evils of dope. I simply don't feel like it. I am just not tempted. I have an attitude towards dope similar to people (I've met them and previously never understood them) who've tried it but 'it didn't really do much for me…didn't like the taste…', plus I have a casual 'if that's what people want to do, well…..that's their choice,' attitude i.e. there's no frisson between me and it. I recognize the handwriting (my notes on the 12 steps) i.e. the smell, but I am minus the connection with the old thoughts about dope and don't therefore have to make any effort to short circuit them. They're simply gone. The idea of me smoking weed now just seems a bit silly, which it is. I now struggle to see why I felt so strongly otherwise. We can change.

Don't get me wrong, the journey from dope being my one piece of buoyancy I clung to alone in the Ocean of Despondency to 'smoking weed now just seems a bit silly', is beyond adjectives. And the note to self here is that I have always needed to be addicted to something, drink especially, and gambling less so, were always swimming along side, plus others which in the main were destructive in nature; now I live a life of moderation, the idea of which in the past would have revolted me. I guess its part of being grounded and centered.

I can't be alone in this philosophy about staying away from the addictive behavior before one can be cured. Rehabilitation clinics subscribe to this I believe, they are strict about it from what I gather. And what I am saying is: to get cured, go beyond dealing with the festering sore, dig out the cause. It is likely there will be layers to go through requiring consistent application of self honesty in order to dig down. Or you may go directly to the cause of the trauma and re-expose yourself to it, face into it and work your way upwards through the layers the trauma created; layers that seem, at times, to endlessly keep multiplying, fragmenting and reappearing in different shades. You may choose to fix the negative behaviors caused by addiction, and sort the root cause at the same time: a simultaneous top down and inside out approach. And that's just the cerebral angle. Don't forget the bodywork too….

Put far more eloquently in a talk I watched on-line featuring a survivor and ex-addict, and a lady well versed in Eastern remedies –

The former said dealing with addiction is more than just chopping at the branches: it is about getting to the root causes. And the lady suggested it is about nourishing the roots and seeing what grows.

I like both plant analogies.

Remember: the addiction may have served you well. It had its purpose. It was necessary in order for you to survive. Now it is time to let it go.

A lot of recovery from trauma is about 'letting go'. When doing the 12 steps as mentioned, I repeatedly wrote the same script on some of the subjects. One was about the concept of 'letting go'. 'Letting go' as I saw it, was not for me. 'Letting go' was passive. 'Letting go' would lead to a weakening of my armour and leave me vulnerable to victimisation. My survival was about not being a victim in life. 'Letting go' didn't fit and was to be ignored. I was right to an extent, but 'letting go' I later found, had a broader application which became very useful, essential.

I discovered the concept of 'letting go' (of a negative behavior pattern for example) is often easier than dealing with the fear of the void left after 'letting go'. Fear of what may fill the void, the fear of feelings lying in wait that maybe evoked; fear of the unknown, the fear of vulnerability. Hey hold on, better off doing and thinking the same thing over and over, it's much safer.... [stay with me on this one – I'll try to explain later].

Accept three things: fear is a hologram: we are by nature creatures of habit: safety is our strongest motivator.

I feared letting go of my addiction.

They won't be nailing me to no cross. I 'lapsed'. Some halfway through the second year of therapy, by way of giving a time scale to it, dope came into my life via a friend and I took it. I figured I was cured and a treat was in order. I even recognized this as a self con. But the voice of addiction finds different guises. The voice of addiction can find a way of talking to you such that you listen, speaking from its grave on this occasion!

This 'treat' concept (it was supposed to a 'one off' – yeah right) was nothing but an excuse. There is no denying it. Brutal self honesty stepped in and told me I was finding an excuse. My therapist concluded I was like a soldier emerging from the jungle warfare of recovery after nearly two years and flopping on the beach to chill, which was true as I did go through a period of exhaustion. But I noticed an element of shame associated with smoking the dope (shame: a useful weapon against addiction, & previously lacking), but I hadn't the energy to beat myself up and we decided it wouldn't help. There's a place for the inner sergeant major and similarly, a place for the self compassion: they have a paradoxical relationship – bear in mind the sergeant's 'tough love' is part of self compassion.

Also noticeably, the effect of the drug was not the same. I instantly wanted the stoned feeling to pass. I noticed how the addictive part of me had to work at getting the addiction going again. I didn't feel that immediate rush coupled with 'hello there, welcome back old friend, everything is going to be okay' feeling. It wasn't the crutch I needed anymore, the desire to numb out; I was drifting back to an unnecessary habit which conflicted with new stuff, not least a freshly discovered array of emotions I was learning to be with, manage and enjoy, plus it clashed with my health kick given I had developed my self worth. Then my wife walked in after being sent by the optician to the hospital and said, 'I've got a brain tumour.' It was an easy decision to be the best I could be from then on so I dropped the 'treat' which had spluttered and coughed along for a few weeks. Some relationships come to an end and there's no going back.

I personally believe you have to stop the addictive behavior before you can truly cure the addiction. This is a contradiction and seemingly overtly impossible

In summary, to conquer addiction the decision has to come from you. Absolutely no one else that ever lived, or will, or is, can take your addiction away. Once you acknowledge your addiction, make the decision you no longer want to be an addict, make the decision you will be *addiction free* (look to the 'go towards' rather than the 'go from' – I am vs I am not), and decide how you are going to live the rest of your life. You will do it. Have faith in your will power, no one else's. Anything else is irresponsibility. You are responsible for you. You have the power to dictate how you live your life, it's already in you.

Fighting addiction can be done with abstinence alone i.e. just stopping. In fact it is necessary (obvs) but you *may* forever feel like a leashed dog. Employing only abstinence may be a hard haul most probably requiring on-going conscious effort. Either way, the necessity of stopping needs to be subsidized with re-direction i.e. finding replacement things to do/consume that are more positive than the addiction in order to create new habits and subsequent new neural pathways which in time, when coupled with self discipline, become easier and easier to follow. Also, changing a habit also involves a load of periphery stuff like getting the buy in of people around you i.e. a support network (12 steps/

‘group’/friends/family), and switching out people who perpetuate your addiction: peers have a massive influence on your behavior. This is dealing with the addiction at a behavioral surface level. This is part one, the action part, of the two part conscious ‘top down’ approach as I call it.

The second part of the conscious top down approach is wielding the scalpel of self honesty and adopting true reflection in order to change behavior patterns, not just those directly connected to the ‘doing’ of the addiction. It’s about employing brutal honesty about what the addiction actually does: its net effect on you, your life and those around you. Getting real about what happens to you and how you feel when you are up, when you are down, and the in between. What do you truly project to others? What are they really thinking and feeling about you as an addict? What are you truly thinking and feeling? What actions are you taking and not taking? What are you in denial about? What is the total price (well beyond the fiscal aspect)? What are you going to do about it? What conscious active changes are you going to make? Not just to the behaviors associated with doing the habit e.g. the ‘scoring’ of the drug or going to the pub, the part one stuff, but also the behaviors resulting from the effects of the habit, including the behaviors during indulgence, after, before, and behavior created by the addiction in relation to others and the World in general i.e. the manifestation of your addiction onto others.

Conscious Top down: 1. Stopping the habit. 2. Stopping the associated & resulting behavior.

Along with the top down approach is the inside out process which can be done at the same time i.e. looking at why you are an addict: digging to the root cause, the trauma if it be so. This, in a sentence, is about recognizing, understanding and feeling the effects of that trauma if necessary over and over, which is easy to say but not to do, i.e. experiencing how trauma held inside radiates feelings and subsequent thoughts which you have been numbing out with addiction. By sitting in those feelings their hold on you will weaken and with that, the need to numb out (addiction is escaping from oneself, not the World).

The last two paragraphs, in essence, are the backbone of this book, and are the backbone (in my opinion) of the process of conscious recovery from trauma.

And **NB** I am proposing this methodology to 'addiction' in its broadest interpretation i.e. *any* behavior pattern that you recognize does not serve you and is destructive to you and/or others.

Key is: 'ownership' of behavior.

BTW - The cost of failing to treat the trauma of childhood abuse in addiction can be immense, leaving survivors vulnerable to relapse. Public Health England estimates the economic burden of alcohol related harm alone is approximately £25bn to £50bn each year (PHE Annual Report & Accounts 2016/17). In 2014 The National Treatment Agency estimated the overall annual cost of drug addiction was around £15.4Bn/annum. £13.9bn due to drug related crime (roughly the cost of building 40 large hospitals, every year!)....

So tell me, what else do we need to know before we ***all*** *decide that we are going to eradicate childhood abuse?*

The birth right of every child is safety. It takes a village to raise a child.

****

My wife and I were lying in bed about 8.30 one autumn morning waiting for the other to get up and make a cup of tea when the phone rang, the landline, which was unusual. We'd recently returned from living in New Zealand with only suitcases so had only basic furniture. I drew the short straw, went downstairs and picked up the phone from the floor.

'Hello.'
'Hello, it's Mark.' I knew it was Mark before he said 'Mark'. We'd known each other since we were five. Typically, he'd know I knew it was him: before speaking he always took a distinctive imperceptible in breathe I'd immediately detect, and he would just say 'aaup, owyadoin?'
Not this time. Of the hundreds of times he'd called since we were little boys he never once said, 'Hello, it's Mark.'
Neither would he call this early. He was not a morning person he knew I knew, and neither am I which I knew he knew. This was proper serious. He had something he didn't want to say.
'Go on mate,' I said steadily by way of encouraging him. I'm ready. I wasn't.
A momentary pause, we braced; another in breath.
'I've got some bad news. It's Rich, he's hung himself.'

****

2. Suicide

I had to stop before I began to write. I tried to think of why I haven't committed suicide; trying to decide if there was an underlying reason I could project either about me, my life or what I have learnt, forming the one factor stopping me from having killed myself so I might pass it on. I always believed some people are destined to kill themselves and I was one of them. I never transcribed this onto Rich. I never considered it in terms of who else might kill themselves; I simply accepted I most probably would. Not a question of 'if' but 'when'.

I never discussed the idea of killing myself with anyone previously, except with my wife on one occasion some twenty years ago and a therapist I saw when I was twenty nine, until I got severely depressed prior to my breakdown when most days my wife made me promise I would be alive when she got back from work.

Thoughts of suicide have haunted me all my life, but they didn't always arrive packaged the same way. There wasn't a set pattern. The realisation I needed to end it didn't come from a given direction with the same signals in advance. I label the feeling of suicide as 'the suicide snake' with chameleon qualities. The suicide snake can change and adapt like the voice of addiction.

I said 'except my wife on one occasion' because I tried to convince her we should commit double suicide. I, to this day, know I would find life so hard without her and I didn't want to leave her alone; I wanted her to come with me. The point is: at that time we lived on a sand spit splitting the Pacific Ocean from a huge beautiful harbour with the most spectacular landscape all around. We both had comfortable jobs and an idyllic lifestyle. I reasoned it was not going to get any better, we had made it to our pinnacle and life from then on would be a disappointing compromise which I knew only too well, and we should kill ourselves. I felt we were living on that sand spit metaphorically, either side was a void of unknown most of which would be desolate, and moreover, despite living an idyllic life I still wasn't happy. I had formed a line of reasoning perfectly logical and conclusive. Being a survivor I used to be haunted by a subterranean sense of doom which became acute when I noted that although life was great it was always present with its inescapable gravity. If she had been agreeable I do think it a real possibility I would have pressed ahead. Just take a massive dose of sleeping pills and both lie on the bed I figured – Sophie's Choice. She reacted much the same way as I would now, 'don't be ridiculous,' and wouldn't brook any argument. But at the time I was serious.

The suicide snake can be so convincing with its logic and ability to close off all the exits. I am attempting to express that suicidal thoughts engulfed me in different ways at different junctions in my life, during the outwardly good times and bad. This may be why 'people don't see it coming' when someone they know takes their own life. Rich had spent the weekend before with his immediate family and appeared fine. Life for him, on the face of it, was the best it had been. His older brother, who attended the scene, told me that most probably the last thing Rich looked at was his six year old daughter's bicycle. He absolutely doted on her. I had met him a couple of months earlier; he had photos of her and him from their adventure to the Glastonbury festival in his prized vintage VW camper spread out on the table in the pub, and enthused like never before about the work projects he was involved in.

Oh Rich, you are loved so dearly.

The suicide snake has visited me many times. It got me good when I was twenty nine. I was in a good job with a great social life. Again, on paper everything was fine but I wasn't happy, I just felt empty. 'So this is it then?' I just looked ahead at a forsaken future, always stuck being me. I felt total despair and saw logically there was no hope for me, I just wasn't meant to be alive. But I figured I should reach out. I remember going through the phone book, it was a Sunday and reasoned I'd make one phone call to one therapist and if it didn't work for whatever reason I would get on with it and kill myself. Label it coincidence, whatever, a man did answer and invited me to talk to him right then. He used hypnotherapy as part of his process which I found very effective, in fact if I were to go back to therapy it would be method I would consider. He was also well versed in the effects of childhood sexual abuse, and during the few sessions we determined my being abused at some swimming baths by a stranger when I was a young boy had affected me. I was reticent to fully acknowledge the effects but we made progress and I did process them to an extent,

'..oh, it was just something that happened…' (I packaged it away)...

The work we did helped for a good few years. We didn't directly address that I had been abused at home, other than discussions around a childhood of neglect, taking until recently to manifest fully in my conscious mind despite having had flashbacks. I had subconsciously and consciously suppressed the memories by way of a survival tactic, and remained in denial by way of preserving the 'ideal' I wanted to believe my childhood was; the foundation of me which I could label, bury and forget (and escape – having deserted the UK aged 22), consequently they didn't fully surface until much later in life. This is common. There are various figures broadcast all suggesting it is usual for the survivor of childhood abuse to consciously recognize they were abused and begin to process it many years later (average 25 to 30 years to declare and begin to process, it is said).

Another documented fact is that abusers can spot neglected children.

How about we add the most important people on Earth (children) to the equal human rights list?

ALL GP's and counselors and therapists should be looking for any history of childhood abuse with people that are enduring emotional and therefore mental distress. 1 in 4 females & between 1 in 6 males experience childhood sexual abuse – add in violence, neglect.... All have a direct negative impact on emotional and mental health throughout their lives. It is proven that people having endured childhood abuse are more likely to endure mental health issues..... Therefore the person that declares they are enduring mental distress....what is the chance they are a survivor of childhood abuse...50/50?

That hiss of the suicide snake. Oh, how it can change and adapt. How that snake can gently and insssidiously weave its way towards you, bringing its comforting coldness, a familiar chill, dissipating your hope, offering balm to confusion, to angst, depression, shame and self hatred.

'There is an answer,' says the snake, 'you know I am the ansssswer. I can see you, you know we are close you and I, I understand you, you know that, why resisssst?'

The snake coils around you whilst you submit to its comforting clarity.

'Now is the time. This time, fool your self no more,' the snake clearly hisses. 'They don't care, they don't really care. They can't think past themselves in this empty soulless World of hopelessness. You don't need to be part of this lie anymore,' the snake beckons.

'They don't need you, with your 'you' anymore. That you, that useless you, that shell that is you. Your life is a lie. You are a lie and they know that, they humour you. You are alone. There is nothing, just you and the pain. The forever pain. Stop it all now. That's enough now. Time to go. Time to move on. We know better than thisss don't we?' explains the snake with its perfect logic.

'There is nothing here for you except hopelessness and doom. The snake will save you. The snake will save them. Save them from you: that shameful empty you. It's time to leave all thisss. There is no point in this anymore. It doesn't make any sense does it? Where is the sense? Isn't sense just foolishness, isn't it, yes, you know it is' hisses the snake with calm.

'There is only one sense. Only one senssse to it all and you know it. It's been there all along.' The snake coils around you and you pant and feel angst as the moment comes with its absolute clarity.

I have paced about or sat staring into the middle distance so many times at four in the morning when the World is asleep, wrestling with the snake. As the sense of despair grew the option of suicide would loom ever clearer.

I was probably most susceptible when life became a flame I could huff out with one puff. Life could be dropped like a small sweet wrapper, that 'hey, in the big scheme of things compared to the Universe' really was just that, a now done with one inch square sweet wrapper I could drop. I meant to put it in my pocket but it slipped through my fingers with a tiny flinch and I didn't pick it up, or think of it again. And some people might grieve a little, but they will carry on, as would the rest of the silly insignificant World and I, like the sweet wrapper, would just…be gone. Suicide was simple. Suicide became obvious. Starkly obvious.

But I decided not to kill myself. I knew at my core was hope alloyed in defiance: this was my only weapon, the only weapon I needed.

Sometime later when Mark and I were having a giggle we took a breath and reflected on Rich, wishing he were with us and wondered why he'd done it. Mark, often capable of pure incision, said 'for him at that time it made perfect sense.'

Yes. Yes, of course. Of course it did. Of course, yes, for him at that time. Yes, perfect sense. Yes of course, for him at that time, it made perfect sense.

Not later, not after, not at all. No sense whatsoever.

I've had a close relationship with and interest in suicide. I've heard stories by people who attempted suicide and not died; not 'cry for help' deliberate failures. I recall a man telling about jumping off a specific bridge which has a history of being the end of several people but he miraculously survived, and he said, as did all other survivors of suicide attempts whose stories I heard, that he experienced a moment of absolute clarity just before he knew the end was imminent, i.e. their last moment of conscious recognition, it was one of absolute regret: they shouldn't have done it. Not resigned calm coupled with 'oh good it's going to end'. Not one.

Most people don't consider committing suicide. They probably think it a very strange concept. I don't know what people who never consider suicide think of suicide and of those that do it. Some people say it is selfish, others reason it is their life and their choice to make. I am of this latter way of thinking, but my attitude to suicide has changed. This is because I no longer have suicidal thoughts. I'll qualify a little further. Suicidal thoughts do present themselves occasionally or, more accurately, the suicide snake is safely tucked away in its basket i.e. considerably reduced potency of suicidal thoughts, and I have mechanisms, the charmer's flute, to deal with them.

Watch the clip of Jungle Book (1967- my fave childhood film) when Shere Khan [the tiger] meets Kaa [the snake] and holds it by the throat, and when the snake tries to hypnotize the tiger gets its head instantly slapped to the ground.

'....I've no time for that sort of nonsense...'

Since my breakdown and subsequent recovery which I recognize is on-going; my attitude to suicide has changed and is less clear cut than it was. If I hear or read about a suicide now I feel deeply saddened. I empathise with how they may have felt; the only thing left to do was to end their precious life.

The main weapon against suicidal thoughts is reaching out. Suicide is a lonely act. It is likely they have brewed up to it. For onlookers the act appears to be carried out on a whim, but it is likely the person has been harbouring suicidal thoughts, even if they waver, magnify and shrink. I believe it is unlikely someone takes their own life the first time they think of it. To commit suicide is a big decision. I have studied how and why people make decisions and typically it takes several exposures to a big idea before people move forward and take action.

The suicidal thoughts came during my breakdown…*'breakdown': by my definition was a feeling of hitting a wall, of no longer being able to function in any way matching my past. I was unable to do basic things like, as a good example, go to a supermarket which involves a stream of decisions none of which I could manage e.g. write a list even. I'd be wracked with so much angst I couldn't go out, couldn't transport myself to the supermarket and certainly not achieve anything there because I wanted to sob every half an hour for half an hour...prompted by the feeling, 'I just can't go through this. It is too much.'*…the suicide snake openly attacked full on and squeezed and squeezed. I had to phone my therapist, it was the first time in my life I felt I was beaten. I was screaming for help. It was like a powerful drug had engulfed me. I became really frightened because I couldn't stop or fight the feeling. I was overwhelmed. I'd lost. I was going to kill myself. She was amazing. We'd had some difficult times but when I was drowning she saved me. She held me up. She saved my life.

I am seeking to identify a couple of points I hope will be useful. If you've had suicidal thoughts I suggest getting a strategy in place ready for their return. Chances are if you've endured trauma, and this is the root cause of your suicidal tendencies, unless you are serious about processing the trauma and getting past the effects, suicidal thoughts may re-visit.

What would be the elements of a strategy? Firstly, let me say that having a strategy is, by its own definition, a weapon of deterrent. Knowing you have previously made a conscious plan will by its very existence dilute the suicidal thoughts. The suicide snake slithers up when you are feeling weak; having a strategy to implement is an antidote. You won't have to fight or reason with the snake as much given you have a plan worked out in advance.

The first thing is to see the snake coming, despite its various guises and nuances of communication [*it will find a code that is pertinent to you; it will use your language]*. There will be warning signs. Suicidal thoughts don't pop into one's head by surprise, so don't ignore them. Better to head off the snake early: be ready to stamp on it. Be ready with positive things to do when the snake slithers towards you. Or make a change, do something new. Treat yourself (with something positive, not destructive escape) without stretching things e.g. your finances, which will cause regret later. Stop and think, 'I've had suicidal thoughts before, so what am I going to do? I am going to recognize and acknowledge the signs. I am going to do stuff about it. I am going to do positive stuff for me that I enjoy doing.' Back to Aldo and getting your feet up. Anticipate.

Also, speak out, very important. When that snake coils around and the essence of your spirit evaporates and the venom infuses depression, get help. Plan in advance who you will talk to, make an agreement with someone/s (preferably 'someones' - plural) you can talk to. Tell people in advance you get depressed and may need to chat. Get agreement in advance from folk you can call. I say 'someones' because it is better to spread the load. It's not fair to repeatedly dump on the same person when things aren't going well. It takes work to give support, so asking in advance is the way. When we are open with people and ask for help they usually offer what they can, they want to. But consider what you will do if your one person is inconvenienced when you are backed into a corner by the snake? It's unfair to expect them to drop what they are doing purely because you shout for help. They have busy lives. People want to help but it is probable they have to disengage from a pattern in order to support you i.e. make a sacrifice, so don't expect too much of people. And it is better to send a flare to several folk thereby spreading the burden, plus, sharing with many gives different perspectives and broadens your thinking. You don't realize when truly considering suicide that your perspective on life, your situation, is narrow and it often takes someone else to widen it. Sharing lightens your burden and helps get a different viewpoint. And talking is a great release.

'…a problem shared…'

Let me cite an example of broadening perspective.

Of the members of the extended family I told about being abused as a child my older cousin Mervyn believed me (being believed is essential). Previously, we hadn't interacted much, the odd family 'do's' etc. I have lived overseas a lot and whilst in the UK we were many miles apart, had different lives. He stepped up when he heard of my breakdown and the cause (my breakdown was triggered by his brother's death in Australia- the big one that stayed at Xmas). He was a rock. Like I said, it is surprising who gives support when you need it. We met a few times in London, he came to see me and we had some really soul nourishing afternoons together. We shared a lot and became close. I grew to love him and was deeply grateful for his support.

I got a call: he contracted meningitis on a Thursday and by the end of Sunday they had switched the life support machine off.

His passing was particularly significant for me. Six months earlier Mark (my little childhood friend and joy) also passed away suddenly and unexpectedly.

I was just beginning to see daylight after the Tsunami of my breakdown. I was beginning to function. Both these significant events really served to push me under. Had they happened a year earlier total misery would have overwhelmed me, a perception that foundation stones in my life were destined to be taken away. As if the snake were playing chess with me and was going to win: taking my key players off the board and cutting down my options, hemming me in.

I did grieve so heavily. When Mark passed I called my therapist for, to be fair, only the second time. By agreement we had previously ended our meetings after one year but again, she was so exquisitely crafted in the way she helped me accept the pain and she gave me the faith in myself to be with it. A year earlier I would have decided the World was against me and decided these two catastrophic events were part of the design to break me, occurring in order to force me to grasp the concept that life was hopeless. But I had moved on from this 'destiny of doom' thinking. I knew the two significant deaths would be very, very hard to accept; to this day I think of them both and miss them dearly, often conversing with them. Now I must grasp life ever the more.

A more immediate change of viewpoint and gaining new ones via sharing came to me after these terrible events in my life, and was spawned by Merv's funeral. I didn't sleep before. Alone I arrived early and on approach to the church noticed several people milling about whom I didn't have the where with all to mingle with, so I went to a café for a quick cup of tea. On my return everyone, bar a few stragglers, had filled the church and I was confined to a back row in a corner, a good distance from the entrance, causing a self conscious journey to my seat far from members of the family (the church didn't have a traditional layout of an entrance with a main corridor down the middle and two sets of pews either side). At the end of the service, being trapped in a corner, I missed the cars carrying the family to the crematorium, instead I went to the wake attended by many, none of whom I knew. I wondered about feeling isolated and disassociated. I left, walked about the town feeling conspicuous in a black suit and tie, and then went back. The family still hadn't returned from the crematorium. I couldn't cope. I felt lost, forlorn and angry with myself, so I left.

I didn't typically talk about 'things that happened this last week' with my second therapist unless they provided windows to something bigger. But I felt so guilty for not sitting it out and waiting for Merv's wife and family. I wanted to do the right thing. I felt cowardly and noticed I wanted to obsessively beat myself up about my behavior. My therapist expounded that adult rational me had taken the hand of my little Gregory and angry Greg, and made the wise choice of getting them home. I had done the right thing. I also explained what happened to my friend Malik, who impatiently fiddled around with bits of paper whilst I spoke, and when I'd finished he instantly asked if I had gotten into a fight, to which I replied indignantly that I hadn't, so his take was I had gone and paid my respects and not got into a fight, so it was all good!

I hadn't considered either of these viewpoints: guilt gone - reframing.

Just giving an example of how getting different perspectives from others is helpful. Helps you get movement. This is an entirely new methodology for me, having been conditioned from childhood, 'you're on your own fella, trust no one'.

Suicidal thoughts are often accompanied by shame, as though having suicidal thoughts is shameful. My own view was narrow; talking about depression and suicide would be declaring a weakness and a self indulgence I wasn't entitled to. For me, raised to suppress my feelings, 'What have you got to be depressed about?' would be the mother's dismissive response on either of the two occasions I ventured to express my woes to her, I certainly wouldn't risk expressing vulnerability to the narcissist father empirically knowing it would be ridiculed and used against me at a later date.

Men are more likely conditioned to view expression of feelings as weakness, and expression of suicidal thoughts as an admission of defeat.

Wrong. Narrow thinking.

Vulnerability is strength. It takes strength and courage to be vulnerable.

Use professional services. Have them at hand. Make the decision that if the snake gets a hold you will make the call; you will give them a chance. If you ever considered suicide then how about making that decision now, before the time comes? Make that decision now whilst you are feeling balanced and ok. Then it's done. You don't have to wonder what to do when things go out of balance, you've already decided: you have a plan. Yes…make sense? It does, doesn't it?

Feeling suicidal? Time to dig in to yourself – it's simply a warning light flashing from within. You are telling yourself to get help; you need to talk and share. It could well lead to the discovery of you. You will be delighted with what you find, have faith.

3. Not Recovery

Recovery from trauma and/or mental health conditions does not follow a linear path i.e. stage one you do this, stage two you do that etc. I say it again: your journey is your journey. It is, and has been, exactly right for you. Where you are at right now is exactly where you are meant to be.

To not recover is recovering. There is a very useful purpose to holidays. We need them. I sense when I'm too intense with my journey, when it becomes a way of life, when all I think about and all communication becomes centered on recovery. Fortunately my partner points this out and brings all sorts of features to the airwaves, not least tales of others enduring more difficulty than I have experienced certainly in my adult life (which evokes *gratitude*), bringing my awareness away from this inner journey which can become self absorption and paradoxically, not healthy. The purpose of the journey of recovery, perhaps on-going, is that the process blends with life and makes life easier, healthier, and enables the person to 'be' with inner peace. One has to stop and smell the flowers.......You can stop trying to resolve everything and give it space.

I have taken a back seat from a group I have been a very active part of just now, and I'm consciously not reading about mental heath conditions, or looking for information or stories about CSA. Plus, I am consciously taking the trouble to connect with people that don't have CSA or mental health on their agenda (got folk out the drawer).

Being totally immersed in 'recovery' and having everybody around you involved in recovery and mental health issues can become inhibiting. I have to be aware I listen to a sergeant major voice inside me too much (not an actual sergeant major's voice, or even a voice as such), berating me for not constantly working at recovery.

Be aware of becoming addicted to your own issues which is easily done. So called 'dealing with' mental health issues becomes a way of life, a choice I guess. My feeling is there is more to life than dwelling on your problems, and the idea of facing into the issues is to make living better: the 'living' being all the horde of other bits and bobs having nothing to do with mental health.

The abuse, the trauma, doesn't define us.

Let's stop and stress this point: the causes of any mental health issue, or issues, we may be dealing with do not define us. It is not the whole of us. It is a husk.

Taking a break from dealing with my mental health is good for my mental health.

'Not recovering' might also be acting in a fashion you are trying to alter. You may view this as a step backwards. You may feel guilty for doing, behaving, saying stuff, you were trying to change or stop. You previously recognized a pattern and recognized its cause, understood it, owned it etc, but repeated it anyway causing a feeling of despondency, as though self defeat is hardwired in and although conscious of a negative routine, you still can't stop it.

Chill.

What advice you would give to someone inflicting self criticism e.g. 'I should know better', 'I've let myself down' etc, for some perceived misdemeanor?

You'd say 'give yourself a break'. At least they acknowledge it, and that's all they need to do right now.

'Hey come on, we are all human.'

Control was one of my safeties e.g. doing everything perfectly and expecting everyone to adhere to my unspoken rules of behavior; I struggled to grasp that we are flawed so often duff things up.

'We are human.' Give yourself and others plenty of wiggle room.

My friend and I were busking and a delightful young lady invited us to play at her engagement party. It went really well. I play sax but also have a collection of maracas and shakers. I typically feel that big Greg plays the sax whilst little Gregory plays the maracas. On the way back sitting on the underground I looked across at my exotic busking partner from the Congo donning one his especially bright outfits as we left what was a new area of London for both of us, the whole night having been a magical adventure, which we even got paid for; a glad to be alive, special night. We parted on a platform where we both changed trains and I sat down on the next one and gazed. I became conscious I was staring at a young man opposite me, but I must have been somewhat unfocused. I half consciously realized, given his manner, he registered my look as threatening because his face took on an aggressive tone. He later looked inquisitive, he could see me looking stunned and that I wasn't thinking about him, I was just using his eyes as an anchor. His look changed to sympathy. My eyes had welled up. I had left my bag with the maracas on the other train. All the multitude of times when I have managed to consciously or unconsciously shoot myself in the foot stood around me in a big circle and yelled at me. The World was against me. No matter what I do, how good it gets, I will not be allowed to enjoy it; I am not worthy. That crippling sense of unworthiness CA survivors, especially, often carry around was released, exaggerated by the feeling I had let my inner child down; I had trampled on his spirit as my parents had repeatedly done. It proved he was not really safe with big Greg either.

The serpent of doom hissed at me.

This event took some getting past. Fortunately, I was a good way into therapy equipped with a supply of new tools plus a new way of thinking: a method by which I could ***choose*** *a different path of thought. It was severely tested at this juncture. I felt the familiar sense of defeat begin to swamp me, but now I could choose differently. I could stop the helter skelter into what could be deemed as self pity and the descent towards the abyss...... Allow me to jump to the part of the story that is relevant right now: I went to the lost property unit sometime after navigating the TFL lost property website (which I hasten to add, even my hyper neurotic ultra picky outer critic at its uptight worst, which it especially was on this occasion, could not find fault with) armed, I thought, with a load of good karma because when I find things I always hand them in. At the HQ of TFL lost property on Baker Street what struck me was the size of the operation, staff, computers and software, warehouse and systems etc. The point is: loads of people lose loads of things all the time (a lot of which would be important to them)! I explained this whole saga to Merv on one of his visits of support to which he retaliated with a story about his recent trip to South*

America to climb a mountain, having trained extensively and made in depth plans for, but left his valuable camera, which he had researched into and saved up for and bought especially for the adventure, on a chair in the café in the airport. Merv was the most adult together person I've ever known! I genuinely felt for him and empathized entirely with that moment when you realize what was important has gone, but I admit I was also a bit relieved.

The point of the point is: we all make mistakes!

We lost objects……….only. They are not symbolic of something deep and meaningful. Yes, if we constantly loose things, which I used to….okay, that points at something…not being in the present… perhaps…because….but otherwise, be patient with yourself and let go…you are human like everybody else and not as different as you think.

The route to recovery is different for us all. But there are a surprising and reassuring number of similarities which group work bring to light, even though your path will not exactly mirror another's. You may seemingly 'drop the ball', 'lapse'. But I don't see re-enacting the same scenarios as a step backwards anymore. Once aware I'm repeating a negative destructive pattern of behavior, or way of thinking, prompting the inner critic to jump in with the tired script of 'oh no, I don't believe it, I'm xxxxxing again, I can't get anything right, not even this recovery business', I counter by accepting that revisiting old patterns is part of the journey, albeit I now choose to observe the enactment of the pattern mindfully, thus diluting its intensity. In other words, part of having a break teaches me I can treat recovery as flexible, I can step away from stuff. If I 'regress/lapse' it's ok. I needed to. Via observation I can learn from the repetition and choose to diminish the effect of destructive self judgment and subsequent negative feelings about myself. I now have a choice of routes I can take. I acknowledge the existence of choice and I observe myself putting a chosen route into effect, instead of directly plugging in the compulsion to spiral down the slope of self loathing because I 'failed'. As for the maracas, I simply accept that I and everybody else loose stuff and we get a bit upset about it, and then we move on (and buy some more, better ones – which I did, because I am worthy!)

Perhaps Bob and his therapist were right, I can get JT out and urinate and feel ok!

Or rather, recognize making a choice of behavior as being resilient.

As my journey progresses more and more I am taking a light gentle touch with myself. Perhaps, because I am way beyond crisis, I don't need to employ rigid self discipline to monitor and manage my reactions, therefore more and more I am stepping away from me, i.e. the intense self analysis and the polar expedition approach to my journey. It has become more like when we lived in a remote part of New Zealand where four of us sat in inflated lorry inner tubes and floated down a slow moving river just gazing about, always aware.

4. Medication

This subject has popped up a few times in groups I have been in. Each time it is from a brother looking for advice. That is why I've put the topic in.

The following is probably only useful to those thinking about medication and perhaps those taking medication but are disillusioned. For those taking medication some may be holding and invested in a different end of the stick to the following, and don't want to hear otherwise....the following are very strictly my views as I write...yours may differ and are equally valid.

Disclaimer: I know bordering on zero about prescription psychotropic drugs. I don't really know what I am talking about. Following are my thoughts and they could be viewed as entirely prejudiced founded on ignorance. Any use or non use of pharmaceutical drugs by you has nothing to do with me. If it is a consideration, may I humbly suggest, you get professional advice from, again may I suggest, more than one professional.

Now here's my opinion anyway.

I don't like them.

About the time of my first of the two calls to my first therapist when I was clean (no dope or drink for months) and was falling to pieces, and the pain was suffocating me (I can't start to describe how it felt) and I said to her 'help I can't do this', I also called my GP and asked what she thought about the idea of me taking medication, even just for a limited period. I figured this option was there to be chosen given what I understood to be the statistics on the number of people in the UK taking medication, and I know of folk offered/recommended medication after one general chat with their doctor. But she refused. She said 'no' point blank. She said I would never truly process what was happening and happened to me if I did. I wonder then if she'd had this conversation with my therapist, given the two were in the same small building – I don't know. I did hear myself begin the inner chatter about her not realizing the pain I was in and that everybody else was allowed to take them but I wasn't and again, 'when ***I*** reach out the support is just not there' (my first thoughts), but they were overshadowed by a sense of relief. I felt she had faith in me to make it through; she knew it was tough but I would make it. And I admitted to myself at the moment she gave her reason it was right, I was in part hoping she would say no. So despite protestations in my head I was able to cast them out and stick with the programme i.e. recovery. Her 'no' gave my journey the certainty I required. No way out, just forward and victory. But it was a big call on her part, the option of suicide was still on the table. However, my *decision* to recover was reinforced

Point is: I am not 'above' the idea of using medication. I reached, even if partially, for them myself. And what was smoking dope habitually all about if not medicating?

The fact is: I am resilient. Not just physically but mentally and spiritually too. I didn't know this as much as I do now. I owe, to an extent, the newly discovered inner strength to abstinence from medication. But, I am not everybody. Another CSA survivor I considered tougher than me came off her medication, just couldn't do it, and went back on. It could be, and this point is acknowledged among mental health professionals, the effect of withdrawal is worse than the mental state before medication. They need to cold turkey through the withdrawal from the medication i.e. a user needs to go further down before they can re-adjust and come back up. She told me she won't go through the withdrawal and accepts a life requiring medication, and is not fazed by this. Hey life is too short, why suffer? Her call.

But, she went to a funeral of a loved one and reported back that she '..just couldn't feel sad...'...hmmm...

Does medication disable feelings costing empathy for others, thereby inducing narcissistic behavior? Similar to botox, it is documented, whereby quashed expression negates recognition of feelings in others....

The point is (and again, my opinion, perhaps shared): the medication does not cure the underlying issues, the drugs simply numb out the negative symptoms. Take the drugs away and the symptoms return. To recover from trauma there is only one way through: you have to experience the pain. You have to experience the anger and sadness and shame and angst and grief and, and, and. One has to experience the pain, sit in it, flush it out, weaken its hold and therefore reduce its influence on your behavior, and therefore your view on the World and yourself.

I am aware that all pharmaceutical drugs (and illicit ones too) have side effects, and they are unlikely to be positive. 'Side effects' are typically negative. It is recognized that a psychotropic drug will alter your behavior, your thoughts, feelings and your perception, and so may well affect you physically in a negative way.

In essence, there will be a price *(not experiencing sadness at a loved one's funeral?)*

A psychotropic drug immunizes from the pain of thoughts and feelings the user is having. They make life easier, easier to bear, fine. But I am of the opinion that these hard to bear feelings are there to be expulsed. I wouldn't have had my breakdown and subsequent recovery if I had just kept on numbing out on dope. I would have continued living in a contrived reality. A reality warped by drugs. My thoughts and feelings and my connection with them and therefore my actions, decisions and interactions would have continued to be buffered by drugs. In the same way pharmaceutical drugs could have affected me.

I surmise one cannot truly process trauma unless one is completely free of any mind altering substances. The use of pharmaceutical drugs simply puts the process waiting to happen on hold, or dilutes it such that one doesn't truly process it. To go through recovery aided by drugs is to only half go through it and forever be dependent on drugs, albeit going off and on them, until the cycle is broken and the person goes though recovery clean.

I get that some (and nearly me) can't do it and need the drugs given the risk of suicide or self harming, for example, is too high if they don't. I read in a heralded book by a therapist, use of drugs works for some in recovery, albeit the qualification and definition of 'some' was nebulous.

On the same adventure I met Aldo back in '87 I also met Oscar the Swedish meditation teacher on route to California to learn about the use of psilocybin (the chemical that gives the hit in 'acid' and magic mushrooms) in relation to curing mental illness (mental distress). I recently (notably 34 years later) skim read a reputable science magazine announcing this as breakthrough stuff i.e. advocating the use of psilocybin (micro dosing apparently) for a limited controlled period to affect the way people think, feel and therefore behave, permanently.

In the future, long term therapy, TRE even, etc, etc, etc may become obsolete, and also annihilate my current thinking about the use of drugs. But, I should be either be in even more mental distress, or one of the most mentally healthy people on the planet given I consumed a lot, a lot (I lived near the Pennines in my twenties where they grew profusely in autumn. We took them daily for months – *but,* with what *intention*?).

NB I am ignorant on the subject. For the record, at this juncture I don't recommend magic mushrooms. I had a couple of bad experiences ending up in hospital on one occasion (shamefully wasting tax payer's money – as an ambulance driver rightfully expressed profoundly in Yorkshire Anglo Saxon) which skews my view. But, as an addendum: a brother, 'out there' in terms of exploring the recovery process, recently micro dosed with magic mushrooms in controlled conditions after much research, and was very positive about the results i.e. he feels good about life, and pointed me towards the fact that there is a lot of supportive research on this subject.

There to investigate and draw *informed* conclusions; should you choose. *We are in pioneering territory.*

Having been around people in the medical profession I suspect there is a considerable amount of 'for profit' pressure to prescribe medication by GP's in the UK (and I am confident this applies to the US too, if not the 'western' World at least). Pharmaceutical companies are largely first and foremost profit driven, as such there is the potential for morality to be blurred, or left as a responsibility for others. Coupled with GP's being under enormous time pressure allocating only minutes of attention to each patient; it is easy for them to write a prescription for that drug introduced to them by that pharmaceutical salesperson. This is a simplistic view but sometimes it pays to be cynical. I am sure another doctor would have offered me some derivative of fluoxetine. My not having medication was down to my doctor. If she had said 'yes fine, I was going to suggest it' I possibly would have subscribed. But she didn't, as I mentioned, she said and I quote, 'you need to tough it out: go through it so that you can process it,' I am glad she did, and that I did. But I wouldn't inflict what I went through on anyone (except the abusers).

It is worth understanding that the psychological effects of psychotropic drugs in the long term IS NOT KNOWN – [FACT].

They thought (and still think I believe) that zapping people's heads with electricity was a good idea (ECT – electroconvulsive therapy). Incidentally, my wife saw this happen when she was a trainee and said it was one of the most disturbing things she has ever witnessed. Uncle John went through this (I could weep).

Take the medication, but there will be a price. I believe the biggest price will be that you never truly recover. However, I reserve the right not to be forever fixed on this opinion, again, mixing the two might work for some.

Yesterday I received my copy (one and only, possibly ever) of 'Therapy Today' (Volume 32: it was a complimentary because I wrote an article about addiction) which is the magazine BACP (British Association of Counselling & Therapy) put out to its members, and weirdly coincidentally there is an article/interview with a Psychiatrist (Dr. Joanna Moncrieff) on the topic of medication.

The interview raised the point that a client could be 'disempowered by medication' believing they cannot survive without it (interpreted into my words). It also affirmed that, in tests, the difference between the positive effects of placebo and chemical laden medication was immeasurable, suggesting the positive effects of the medication could be found 'in the process of feeling listened to and helped', coupled with the addition of the medication made the client perceive they had tangible support/help/a mechanism. In other words, it wasn't what was in the pill it was what the pill represented; its symbolism created the positive result. Additionally, a comment made in relation to medication as a counter to depression: the person may feel better after a period and stop, but 'attribute their recovery solely to the pills beyond anything they have done or discovered, potentially disabling any tools developed, acknowledged and stored for future use should they feel the same way again'. So in effect, every time they feel bad they take pills and are forever dependent. The medication is therefore stunting growth.

Also raised was the issue of withdrawal, which clearly needs to be engineered. It was proposed the client with a desire to come off the 'meds' should seek professional advice and support. The article claimed withdrawal may have side effects, even 'reimburse the client with enhanced negative feelings than they had originally, generating the belief they can't live without the drugs and so go back to them, rather than seeing it through'. I have seen this first hand with someone very close to me (as broached).

I think, in balance, pills should be a last rather than a first resort. Whereas I suspect, given the statistics on the prolific use of psychotropic drugs, the latter is the case.

I re-invented myself as a carpenter in my early forties and taught woodwork to troubled 15-17 year olds ejected from the 'formal' education system. Several were 'diagnosed' with ADHD. It was noticeable when they were on medication because they were so placid. I found it saddening that their natural boisterous spirits were dampened (like Randle McMurphy at the end of One Flew Over the Cuckoos Nest). They were just lads. No different to me and my mates when we were lads. But they had a now fashionable label given by 'someone that knew best'.

Your future, your choice: what you do or don't consume is down to you.

Before I left NZ after six years during my twenties I spent a week on an archeological dig of a Maori fort mid summer. We stayed in tents dotted about; my friend and I got wasted every night. One baking hot morning I was staggering up the steep hill to 'the dig' past a lone tree half way up where a few were resting in the shade before continuing; I went past knowing if I stopped I wouldn't get going again.

Someone shouted, 'There's a Spanish proverb: God says, take what you want, but pay.'

Addendum: my medication hints. Vit B (12 I think it is) for the nerves along with Valerian. St Johns Wort & Vit D for the mood. Chamomile tea for sleep. NB. I recommend getting an old fashioned Tea pot and using leaves + I visit my local herb shop where the people are a mine of information. BUT…BEFORE YOU TAKE **ANY** MEDICATION / INJEST HERB STUFF – CHECK IT IS OK FOR YOU.

5. Space

I love the use of this word when considering behavior, thoughts and feelings. A German brother whom I met at a weekend for male survivors of CSA, and love dearly, introduced the concept of space during a session when a break off group of six were wrestling with thoughts surrounding 'forgiveness' (a big one, a really big one). There was a huge pause in proceedings as we stared into the centre of the small circle we had formed, waiting for collective intuition to offer an answer.

'There's some space in considering forgiveness,' he said in that clear decisive Germanic style. It was just right because he was right.

Perfect. There didn't have to be a yes/no black/white 'this is the absolute answer'. The answer itself could float about, dissipate and reconnect; it could be malleable, it could be patient and wait.

There was no need to have a solution. The solution was the space.

I employ this 'space' principle a lot now. It has been a cornerstone of my recovery. I'll qualify that further. Using the concept of space denotes my evolving into a person now finding life less of a challenge and therefore helps me in a legion of ways e.g. cuts down on my inner and outer critic, reduces anger, disappointment, stops sadness becoming depression, prevents negative impulsivity…there's a list. Employing 'space' is a very, very useful tool. Thank you Nicolas.

I have also read about the space tool in a good book about managing emotions which is currently quite popular, and both my therapists also alluded to the concept of 'space'. I want to describe it simply and clearly.

We all have thoughts and emotions. Sometimes the thoughts start and the emotions follow. Sometimes the emotions start and the thoughts follow. You're informed 'so and so' said something about you at work, your mind quickly grasps this one and dashes into the file room in the brain dragging out notions why 'so and so' said this, provoking feelings like anger or shame. Or someone suddenly blocks you off when driving and you jolt the car, you become fearful and in turn angry, next up your outer critic is in full flight deciding the person who cut you up is a ' xxxxxx' and because they look like a 'xxxxxx', and all 'xxxxxx' people are 'xxxxxx'ers let's face it'…, and on it goes.

You can make decisions to change what you do. You can make decisions to change the way you think and feel. The way you feel about things will change if you decide to change the way you think about things. The way you think about things will change if you decide to change the way you feel about things. You can choose how you think and feel. You are in charge of you. You are the boss. No one else is responsible for what you think and how you feel. Really!

Easy to say [write] though!

Let's look at a simple relatable example of conscious behavioral change by way of using this as a blueprint applicable to other areas of life, i.e. the subject of 'driving' is interchangeable with a myriad of thought and behavior patterns.

I decided to try something new, go into unknown territory signposted 'not getting angry when driving'. There was reticence. How can this be possible? What will replace the anger? Will I be numbed down and not drive so well? Will other drivers take advantage of me and push in front of me? Will they see me as a soft touch, a victim? How am I going to get there if I'm not impatient and on my guard? (excuses). And hey, if I'm honest, I like driving around being angry, it's a habit, it feels comfortable, I don't know an alternative and a surrogate is threatening to the way I am.

But I became conscious I am too easily angered, that I am dialing into the well of anger from the abuse, which doesn't serve me very well. Now I am conscious there is a replacement. I am conscious the alternative will be just fine, better in fact, easier. I am conscious my previous behavior was a habit; I just did it over and over. I am conscious I am afraid of a change into the unfamiliar, the unknown. I am afraid of the unknown because I need to feel safe. Trauma survivors especially seek safety. Safety is perceived to be found in habits, even if the habits are destructive: habits are known and therefore distinguished as safe. I do this habit, I get that result. I know that familiar result so therefore the habit is safe. And adding self honesty into the equation reveals I am addicted to being angry because I feel empowered which serves to perpetuate the circular pattern. The bottom line is: if I am angry I am safe. But in truth, I get angry because I am fearful. I am fearful that if I am not angry I may be vulnerable. If I am vulnerable I may not be safe…..Time to break the cycle!

Okay, I get it: changing behavior takes a good deal of self awareness, self honesty, and thinking through!

NB... did I disclose?...It takes courage to be vulnerable.

If I become conscious I possess a habitual state of being that no longer serves me and is destructive to me and/or those in my life I then employ brutal self honesty, and I have swung the axe. Thud. The giant weed is going to fall. It will take time; many attempts at going back and forth between the old and the new but, with effort, I will accept the new. I will move myself out of the old stinking caravan with dented empty cans of beer, a sink full of dirty plates, cigarette ends on the carpet and move into the plush new apartment because I am worthy.

I am mindful when I drive and now I recognize I cannot control other people's minds, lives and actions. They have as much right to be on the road and in life as me. I and they are just humans. We all lose stuff and go to lost property. We are doing the 'Conga of life', doing our bit but joined together. And 'oopps, blimey, what a daft thing to do…', …ah well, it's happened, its gone by, no need to dwell, no need to engage anger, they are not the abusers in my past…'. I put in the space which itself becomes a habit, just as the usual 'go to's' want to jump in, a breath of space giving the choice, 'do I need to engage the usual suspects?'

(…make a self *intervention...)*

If I immediately grip the stick I become committed to an 'end of the stick' with no way back because I am invested in an 'end of the stick'. So I don't immediately grip the stick, adding space instead, that way I can choose where I grip the stick, how tightly, or if I grip the stick at all. I just look at the stick and pause and make a choice.

It takes work. It takes conscious thought. But I would put money on this conscious mindful change actually, in time, changing the neural pathways, opening up new ones: neuroplasticity. The effect of the trauma is weakening. You have consciously weakened it.

It's worth recognizing symbolic incidents, or moreover, symbolic reactions to what can be everyday events, they are great temperature gauges of recovery.

Previous to my 'enlightenment' I'd be watching a programme I was obviously interested in since it had my full attention (I am in a possessed state – ever observed someone devoured by TV?), and my wife asks some questions. I ignore her. She asks again. I snap a response. A pattern ensues: 'Why is she always doing that? Why can't she just leave me alone? Why is she needy for attention? Why does she need to know about that right now? It can wait can't it?....blah, blah' harps the critical chattering mind monkey. *The mother being complicit with the abuse deeply resented anyone being relaxed and was compelled to destroy the contentment of anybody in her vicinity. The mother had inner turmoil and this needed to be projected.* So I am calmly watching TV and the questions from my wife *plug into the stored up abuse;* the interrogation from the paranoid demanding mother which enhanced the atmosphere of, and actual physical, suffocation I endured. I feel am I being re-abused; I was 'triggered'. My reactions are therefore magnified. Soon I would feel hopelessly forlorn and cascade into being that lonely, repressed sad little boy I was. And my wife would be sulking, so I would start to feel guilty which initiated the process of beating my self up and zoning out the TV whilst obsessively reenacting the conversation in my head wondering where I could have changed it all, then self hatred would infiltrate, and then I would have to go and smoke another joint.

Then I learnt about space. *I learnt to separate the trauma of the past from the reality of now* and I learnt to recognize that I was being triggered, and by what specifically.

Firstly, my wife is not the source of my trauma. In fact, she is the opposite. A person that did you a perceived wrong is not your abuser; they are simply being a human and bumbling along just like me and thee! It is simply an interruption whilst I am wasting my life watching TV. So I add in the space allowing a disconnection from the dwindling well of childhood abuse thereby disabling the pattern and a new way is discovered which I acknowledge, and I have made progress; gliding into the new territory. Hmmm…feels okay, calmer, easier, with no lingering fall out.

Using the space will change a habit: a habit of being.

I suspect, and I could be wrong, this is how well balanced adults behave and react. I'm not sure because I haven't met many and those I figured might be turned out to be inconsistent!

I add in here a referral back to the seminar on racism and negative judgment at the council which is: acknowledging one's first thoughts and reactions, but seeing them as they are i.e. one's first thoughts only, therefore not necessarily to be pursued any further. Next step, how about injecting the space and finding the better ones?

6. Recovery

I do think you have to head for the light. A chap in a group the other day said, 'it feels like I'm in a curved tunnel at times'.

You have to maintain faith.

Recovery is possible. The news is: it will very possibly take longer and will be harder than you first predict. Aldo up!

When my breakdown started in October 2015 I was offered twenty therapy sessions at first and I remember thinking I wouldn't need all of them, but I am still to this day a work in progress. I had no idea how hard it would be. I've done a lot with my life but the journey of recovery has been a vast Odyssey, nothing I have done or experienced compares. But achieving recovery is worth it.

There are tipping points between victim, survivor and thriver. Each is blurred and you can expect to slide between the three. It happens. Accept that. But as you do the work, as you keep moving, applying the self honesty, making the changes, facing into stuff, you can and will slide more often into a state of being a thriver.

When my breakdown first started I wish I could have looked forward to where I am now, it would have been easier to go through the pain knowing I would come through and feel like this. Too often all you see is an endless wilderness of pain, as though careening towards the edge of the World with a dark void beyond. Even after sometime in recovery you can feel dismayed when sensing you have 'lapsed into old ways', often viewing only the continuing climb rather than stepping aside, looking back and admiring how far you have traveled. It takes mindful observation to acknowledge a way of being that is now different to the way you previously felt, thought and behaved. This is valuable: to cast back on the journey offering yourself well deserved praise, from reflecting on a neat bit of vacuuming to cornering the insidious snake of shame or easily saying no to that drink... *(back to the symbolism) ... I used to always have alcohol in the house, a good supply, and I always knew exactly how much and if lager only super strength (supermarket own brand). One morning someway into my recovery journey when tidying up I found a half empty glass of wine, my one glass from the previous evening. I exaggerate not my dear reader, I actually put a small table in front of the sofa and placed the glass on it and sat down and stared at the glass, alone, for an age. I realised I was looking at a minor miracle that would never have happened in the last forty years; in all that time I would never, ever, ever leave a half empty glass and go to bed – it was enormously symbolic. I knew I was recovering from the childhood trauma.*

Again, the use of a journal is helpful: recording your thoughts and feelings by which you can later measure your recovery.

Remember the saxophone huffing and puffing story? How I stopped nearly passing out but couldn't remember when? Often recovery happens like this. You'll find you just don't behave in a given way any more. You don't think like you used to. You don't feel the same way about some stuff. Your beliefs aren't the same; even those you definitely thought were right, held onto and defended. But in some instances you're unable to identify when this happened. It is important to look back and see how far you have come, to recognize these positive changes, to keep clicking the ratchet of progress.

When my journey began a book 'talked to me' about male survivors of CSA. The author re-affirmed that recovery was possible, but I have never seen a definition or description. So, as such, I am going to give you an idea of mine.

Isolating reactions to incidents gives useful insight. Here's one lasting ten seconds but spoke so, so much to me regarding my progress.

I'm on sitting on a fairly crowded London tube. In the past I would have scanned all the personnel and assessed them: anyone looking threatening would be looked over, and I judged and categorized the 'types' on board. I would then stare into the middle distance whilst tuned in to every micro movement. I was, for good reason, hyper vigilant, a common trait among survivors of child abuse: we learn not to trust our environment and stay vigilant in case of attack. But I didn't do all that, instead I sat down and got into my new tube routine of closing my eyes and breathing steadily and deeply (longer exhale than inhale, count 4 in hold 2 then 6 out) and being in the moment; to just sense and be, let things unfold as they will. I don't recall exactly when this transition happened, I just started doing it from time to time and found it was good and safe. The train lurched to a halt forcing a standing passenger to fall on me and put both hands on me to push back up. I felt their breath. In the past this would not have happened because 1. I would have emitted a vibe so others kept their distance 2. I would have seen, even anticipated, the person falling towards me and blocked them. And in the unlikely event of them actually falling right on me I'd have jumped and they'd get a verbal rebuke making the rest of their journey unpleasant, plus I'd check my pockets suspecting having been 'dipped', all accompanied by my inner critic tearing them to pieces whilst my heart pounded. Not this time: I was in the dreamy frame I had come to enjoy. When the person fell I popped in the space and recognized it was an accident; they needed me as a cushion so I was useful, and was even a tinge glad of that; I felt their hands on non-intrusive parts of my body as they pushed away and heard them whisper 'sorry', and I mumbled 'it's ok,' and continued with my eyes closed, not even challenging myself to keep them closed, totally unconcerned or armed with judgment as to who it was and what they looked like. I let it all go in an instant. I paused before I easily slid back to where I was, which I hadn't really left, and felt a Mona Lisa half smile flicker, and in that moment I realized where I had arrived at and I knew that life had become so much easier.

Another moment like this happened when swimming in the Mediterranean, one of my favorite things ever, when I looked at a small fish. Before I tell you about this moment I need to say I have no religious affiliations. I have traveled around a lot and lived in different countries and a significant part of my adventures had a strong religious component: always taking a respectful open interest in, and educating myself about, the religion/s of the people. But I never felt a need to adopt one. I had no religion in my life whatsoever as a child. It wasn't mentioned either positively or negatively. I speculate I've envied religious folk perhaps feeling they had something I didn't or wasn't worthy of possibly prompting anti religious feelings, albeit they weren't very strong. In balance, I figured religion wasn't for me.

A problem I had with the twelve steps was the concept of 'submitting to a higher power' which I viewed as sacrificing control therefore being passive, leading to victimization and also avoiding responsibility i.e. relinquishing responsibility for my recovery to a 'higher power'. I completed 'the steps' several times and most of my recorded responses to the questions changed but the 'higher power' ones did not. No, I would not be recognizing a 'higher power', or doing any submitting to a non existent nonsense that, if did exist, had a lot of shite to justify. There is a complex relationship I have with the concept of 'higher power' including an authority issue, none of which serves to be explained just now....so, back in the Med (was it a dream?)...I have a 'moment'. I walk back up the beach to my wife who is lying on a sun bed reading a magazine through ridiculously big sunglasses beneath a huge floppy hat and she asks 'how was my swim?' and I say, 'good, I found God.' 'Oh' she says.' 'Yes. God,' I say. 'That's nice,' she responds, 'when are we going for lunch, I'm hungry'.

I lay back on my sun bed and figured that yes, I had found God. Perhaps it took that perfect moment for me to see it. I had recognized there is God. I still do. I see God everywhere. I never, ever thought I would say this. I had a moment of clarity in the sea swimming with a little fish (I procured a 'special' pair of swimming goggles that passed an equally exacting list of requirements as the leather jacket). I felt, finally, a sense of belonging. I belonged. I had my place in this World which was mine and there for me and I occupied it, my natural right and purpose was to be me: a sense of wholeness, of complete worth.

I can't describe it any other way.

When I busk with my friend, I see and feel God. People will smile and wave and stop and listen and children dance and people give us tokens, all sorts of people. In 'The

Bush' market there is every denomination of human on this planet and all have given us tokens of appreciation. It is humbling, it is humanity; it is God. To me God can be found in the song of a bird, the laughter of a child, the smell of a flower, the shimmer of the sun on the river, the coolness of the breeze, the people just saying hello. Have a look. Lift up your head and have a look, have a listen, have smell, have an awareness, have a breathe. Remember that connection I talked about in 'group', that connection with humanity: God

I spent several months years ago delivering cars across the US with a spell in New Orleans, and a stepping stone appeared in the form of a book lying alone in the guest house. Written by an African lady who spoke of a belief that God was in spirit all around us '...the spray of the sea on your face on a summers day...' I recall.

Let me tell you something else. I am going to tell you point blank, right at you because I know. I know I know. I have been down to the depths of the abyss of darkness and seen evil, and come back; now I am grateful for every moment life brings with all it's everything. When you were born you are born pure. Your soul is pure. It remains pure. Your soul remains pure. The trauma of childhood abuse only stains the soul, and you can fix that. The natural process is for the purity of your soul to bubble to the surface, to find a way up, to find away to filter through you. All you have to do is let go and let it.

Recovery, put simply for me, is going from an often inescapable state of deep self loathing and shame caused by imploding violent anger added with total distrust of people and despair of humanity producing absolute loneliness and emptiness, to acceptance of the World and a sense of joy to be a part of it. To stop and hear a bird sing, as I just did, and know a small bird has its place equally as I have mine; we are connected by a spirit that, to me, is God.

To go from waking up foggy headed mid morning and for twenty tortured minutes before my first inhalation of marijuana thinking ‘oh no, I’m still me. I can’t do this anymore.’ To waking up knowing I can do it and that I may well catch I sharing a good laugh at least once!

Fear is probably our first and biggest motivator and on the same coin, the need for safety. Recovery is a fearful process; we are going into the unknown. We are facing self truths we will not want to face or accept. We fear letting go, we fear letting go of thoughts and behaviors we know, thoughts and behaviors that do not serve us or those around us, but we know them and see them as safe. We fear that letting go will leave us open to something we do not know. We fear a space those changes will leave. We fear we will be vulnerable and left with our raw feelings which we will not cope with.

‘Let go and let God.’ Say the steps. I get that now. Let go and fall back and have faith, it is already in you and all round you. Drop your ‘weapons’; your addictions, your critic, your anger, your judgment, your shame, your grandiose, your revenge, your disassociation,….

Part D – Emotions

'...I just let the stress leak from the holes in the bucket...',
'...just observing the weather in me, it will change...'
From Jason quotes – nice one! (two)

1. Are they contagious and is there a cure?

Whooeee....emotions.....this is a totally new area for me. Being of a certain age and generation where children were seen and not heard I reserve the right to be dismayed by 'the young people of today'. Until I watched a fly on the wall documentary about a school where the teachers invested in listening to and counseling the young people, as opposed to my senior school where teachers would regularly use violence. The young people possessed inspiring emotional maturity; able to acknowledge and talk about feelings, recognize them, where they came from and how emotions affected their reactions, and further, how their own reactions might impact their peers and make them feel! (Emotional intelligence) I was amazed. I felt an unfamiliar twang I assessed was envy (not, to be fair, one of my many foibles). This is brand new territory for me! Previously, on my emotional song sheet I had; intense anger which would implode causing exhausting self disdain and depression; next up, the highs i.e. adrenaline rushes from high risk activities, then shame and guilt, and finally, an overwhelming sense of hopelessness and doom. In terms of volume there was either right up or right down. Some survivors of trauma talk of only experiencing numbness, an inability to feel anything. I really can't offer any guidance here. I've always sensed I am living on the edge of a volcano ready to emit molten destructive lava.

So, want to learn about feelings? Drop this and drop by a school and have a chat.

Maybe we are finally getting beyond the belief that academic ability is the only measurement of 'intelligence' (see: 'the theory of multiple intelligences' – I subscribe).

And those lads with ADHD (really?) that 'failed' in school because they were expected, despite having zero family or peer support, to sit still in a classroom and listen and read and become academic and conform to the wishes of someone that enjoyed a lot of encouragement and went to University; who in turn is following a system which demonstrates no prior understanding or empathy for the background and environment which shaped these young men. No, the system failed them. The 'village' failed them. We failed them. '...oh and now they're selling drugs and stabbing each other, why is that? Aren't they terrible!' Nature or nurture? The latter. Trust me, they were just lads and with that, magnificent.

When I first began the ride on the gigantic roller coaster of facing into my feelings and feeling them, therefore facing into the trauma, someone made a valid point I've since heard several times: *we all have feelings and they are much the same.* When struggling, you compute only you are in pain, everybody else is fine (on the merry go round) and getting on with life, they are coping quite happily and accepting what is going on….

.....someone else instead of you/me always seems to know the way....

……. you feel separated and isolated from everybody else. Firstly, they don't especially 'know the way' (just like the perception that everybody else had the perfect childhood – they didn't). Right at this moment folk all around you are struggling with some issue or other; a financial problem, a death of a loved one, a health scare, etc. Secondly, most people, at some point, have thought everybody else knows what they are doing when they feel like they personally don't, if that makes sense.

At this very moment loads of people feel exactly like you do. People experience the same array of emotions as each other. Whatever you are feeling it is not new. You will never have a brand new feeling. All feelings possible have been felt by millions of people existing now, before you, and will be experienced by people that will exist (one hopes) after you.

Having feelings is meant to be. This was a new concept for me. When I began experiencing buried feelings from a traumatic childhood they were immensely powerful; when the dam of resistance and denial broke I was flooded, it was terrifying. Being possessed by emotions was alien territory, and when the Tsunami finally passed I was struck by numerous shades of subtle feelings; different tones of anger for example, some derived from a base of shame then others mixed with disdain et al. In summary, a whole new pallet of emotions came to my awareness. I recall outside the cinema asking my wife if she felt like this or that, at different points in the movie and I confessed I 'welled' up a couple of times.

'Yes I did,' she said 'you were meant to. That's what the director of the film wanted you to feel.'

I even double checked with her asking if she thought everybody else in the audience felt the way I did. 'They did,' she reassured. I was having these feelings, they were taking me to places and it was all new. I had been all over the World, done all sorts, now I was having massive and nuanced experiences in a cinema down the road, and everybody else was too. How in the hell were they coping with them I wondered? My goodness, people are going around having all these different feelings, all the time, everyday, up and down, round and round. I was so used to shutting them off, rationalizing them away, numbing them, and there they were, and everybody is having them! Not 'the weak' (my definition of 'weak' has changed) people: everybody. We were meant to, they enrich our lives. My goodness, I get tearful at all sorts of things now. To be fair, often tears of empathetic joy for others or when I experience a spiritual connection which, to me, is God.

I am close to being able to manage my emotions. This is quite different to cutting them off. It is now more about expecting them, being ready for them, being able to sit in them, being with them and....enjoy them by experiencing them!

Sometimes it's good to hear from someone having recently learnt something. It's fresh. I'm pretty sure I couldn't teach someone to play the sax because I'd confuse the pupil given I am disadvantaged by so many complications [although improvising in large part is to let the child within explore and express – is this not living life?]

My first lesson about emotions, which I didn't grasp, came from my first therapist: *sitting in my feelings*. I recollect it may have been during our first meeting when I was leaking a bit: a spit of lava from the caldera, my voice cracking and me welling up.

She stopped me and asked 'what was that?'

'What was what?' I responded defensively, gathering myself, the defenses scrambling into action, the portcullis

slamming down, burners under the oil pot firing up, bowmen to the battlements. I had displayed some emotion!
'Where did that come from?' she asked.
I catapulted a smoke bomb of evasive re-questioning.
'What do you mean', I retaliated somewhat rhetorically.
She pressed on, 'I mean did it come from here?' and put her hand on her stomach by way of example.

I paused and held fire for a brief moment. Perhaps she was trying to get to something.

This was my first introduction to awareness of my feelings.

Acknowledgement of feelings would be self blasphemous. I remember a sense of revulsion at the whole episode. I had betrayed myself by leaking emotions in front of a stranger and now she was highlighting this fact (I suspiciously figured). Consequently, I transferred my sense of ridicule to her by discounting the episode with disdain, claiming she had an unnecessary need to halt proceedings with silliness about a 'feeling coming up'.

By writing the above I visited the distant past. It feels like such a long, long way back now. A flashback to a previous life when I did live in a castle built of 'being right' stone, wore chain mail of ego and blustering, carried a sword of cynicism, knew the Earth was a flat wilderness of distrust, and wouldn't hear otherwise. I don't ridicule myself, I had survived very well, my weapons, tools and techniques having served me effectively, but I needed to move on. It took some doing.

Now I see what she was attempting: awareness of my feelings as they came up. By being aware of them, I would allow them. By allowing them I could feel them and be with them, hold them, go through them and listen to what they were telling me as they passed. And know this was allowed.

But I was very, very afraid of them. They were overwhelming. They overpowered me and I drowned in them and they incapacitated me. They were so powerful and intense, and there so many of them. They seemed to multiply from, at first, the primary colours of the red of rage, the blue of depression, the yellow of angst; they mixed and blended, hid behind each other and changed their guise. I thought they were this but they were that, or something new, or something I thought I knew but found I didn't. They were subtle and lingering, then they wafted through and I couldn't touch them, then they wouldn't go and I would be heavy and exhausted and often feel so old and tired, my will reduced to a wafer.

But the snowdrops did come through.

For a long time, months, I couldn't function. I had to climb into bed every afternoon and curl up and sob incessantly: become my inner child and go through the effects of the trauma. I actually considered it a permanent condition I'd have to manage for the rest of my days. Some brave people go through life with a physical disability, and I figured this was my disability I must learn to live with.

I did listen to her despite my protestation driven by my severe critic and an arsenal of other defense mechanisms.

'Sitting in my feelings.'

The hardest thing I've ever done and I've done some stuff.

I was on this journey, determined to see it through. I couldn't believe how hard it was but I always felt I was lucky, I had three strong women who cared for me in my corner; my therapist, my GP, and my wife.

Incidentally, my GP is the spitting image, visually only, of the mother. There's another book to be written about subterranean spirituality at work – it's not coincidental.

'Sitting in my feelings.' Letting them come up. Oh, how they came up. Wave after wave after wave after wave after wave after wave after ceaseless wave..... never going to stop. I can't do this. This is too much. This is too much even for me. The snake became a giant python so much stronger than me, and held me and squeezed and squeezed and I begged for mercy and it fed on my weakness making it squeeze harder. The panic. The raw panic. The screaming panic. Screeching and screeching and screeching and screeching and...please, I beg you please stop.

My only defense was to let go.

Let go and let them through. Let the anxiety be with me. I would sit motionless monitoring my pulse my heart rate at 160bpm for over three hours solid. Or shaking and convulsing in bed in the afternoon: sobbing so much I made no more sound, my face, ribs and stomach aching. The despair. The desolate despair. The endless dark hopelessness of despair. Bleak, endless emotional pain.

I sat in the feelings. They came up and I would panic. Here they come, the big ones. Medicate. Escape. No, sit in them, they are just feelings, they will not kill me. Let them do their worst. Let me feel the worst. Let the snake squeeze.

'Come on snake, squeeze.' Let it squeeze and squeeze. 'I want to know what you can do snake. Oh I know you can pretend to ease off and lure me into believing it's over, that you are done, and I know that is when you really squeeze, then squeeze again, and then really squeeze, squeezing the hope from my core, and you come back and back and back, and just when I think you've squeezed all you can you squeeze more and then more, and then some more. Bring it. You can't beat me snake. Not now I allow you to squeeze. You know it and I know it, and you know I know it. That's why you will weaken and I will own you.'

'Let go and let God' say the steps.

By allowing the feelings in, sitting in them, experiencing them at the most raw and letting them pass through, they will weaken. Their power over me will weaken and I will have power over them. They will be mine to experience and use as I choose.

By letting go and relinquishing power, I gained it say I.

Own the emotions rather than the emotions owning you.

To recover we have to learn turn into and be with our feelings. Find a safe place and time to go through them and experience our pain. It is very hard, very, very hard. When we are in them, those deep intense feelings, we feel so, so alone.

The primary ones like anger, shame, fear, grief, weaken and eventually they pass. They soak and overwhelm us, but eventually they pass. They pass every time. They do. I've been there. Oh yes, they come back time and time again but eventually, overall, their force weakens. As they grow weaker, we grow stronger. We grow able to be with them. We feel where they sit in our body. We allow them knowing we will go through them and they will weaken, as such we expulse their control over us. We find we are naturally equipped to be with them and process them.

For me, for all the group meetings I've had, the therapy sessions, the books, emails and reports etc I've read, the stuff I've written and all the other recovery things I have done, learning to sit in my feelings is the single most important factor in my recovery.

I recently went through a sad three days. Sadness, unlike anger, can linger for a good while, whereas anger will boil up and boil away (or rather, sink back down and implode). I started to feel depressed. A state of depression for me used to last for weeks fueling suicidal thoughts. So what's the difference now? Firstly I front up, 'hey I notice I am feeling sad': I consciously recognize it. Then I accept I am sad i.e. tell myself it is perfectly okay to feel this way, everybody experiences sadness at times, not just me. I don't try and squash or escape the sadness by doing something or taking something that will numb it. And by recognizing and accepting the sadness it won't own me. I remind myself the sadness will pass. So what am I going to do about it so it doesn't helter skelter into darkness? Am I communicating with enough people? Am I getting isolated? Am I getting enough light? Am I getting enough exercise? I'm stuck indoors so am I giving myself projects to get on with I will look back at and be pleased with? Good, that should help put some lubricant on that sadness so it slides on through. And it will. It will pass.

But the sadness hung about. Let me have a look inside. Okay, is this sinking into depression? It is starting to show signs of it. I feel heaviness in my stomach. I'm starting to get irritable and distant, stuck in thought. I'm feeling tearful, heaviness behind my eyes that persists. So what is going on? I figure something has triggered me. An event can cause us to overreact because it taps into this well of often unresolved feeling we have unconsciously pushed down into ourselves, unresolved.

Identifying a trigger directs me to my past and in turn gives an insight into what, if anything, I haven't exposed to the light and dealt with. I see triggers as opportunities. I read a book recently describing them as 'thorns'. We have thorns we can choose to pull out, or bandage up and spend life being careful not to knock: avoid stuff threatening to disturb them and cause us pain. The latter route, I believe, does not lead to a full recovery and freedom, it condemns to a life whereby one chooses to avoid 'triggers' which proves tricky to navigate causing bouts of pain, inhibiting personal growth and a fully lived life. Plus, having triggers can be a reason to have excuses: 'I can't because it might trigger me.' And worse, harboring triggers evolves to excuses leading to avoidance of responsibility for destructive behavior.

Triggers, as painful as they may be, give insight. They are essential keys to recovery - *(the TV interruption story)*

I went through a period of re-visiting my childhood in as much detail as I could recall, by conscious design, as part of my journey, and on-line I found several pictures of the house I lived in as a boy (it had been for sale in the recent past I discovered). I say 'conscious' because the first journey via therapy into my childhood, beyond actually living it as courageous little Gregory, caused my breakdown and felt as though I'd been dropped ill equipped into a hostile jungle. This time I went back fully tooled up; not to re-expose and re-victimise myself unnecessarily, or by way of going around and around and never moving on, but to really dig out any remaining roots in a planned conscious fashion. In all, this time, I was less disturbed, not forever trying to grasp and accept overwhelming stuff. I was viewing issues objectively; able to choose to observe and manage how I reacted using the space tool in order to be best served by the process. Rather like reading the poem for the second time (and/or being Aldo'd up!).

So, I looked at the house, for the first time for over thirty years. It was helpful. These processes (like declaration) often won't give the reaction I thought they would. I'd guessed I would cascade into old feelings, old wounds; the experience might evoke stuff I hadn't dealt with, re-trigger things. But it didn't. I felt remote and detached. I saw it for what it is now. The house was part of my past but has no hold over me. I have moved on - *'it is just a husk.'*

I was able to 'let go'.

2. Fear

I sent out this email to my wonderful brothers and they liked it and when I said I was writing a book they wanted me to put it in.

Brothers,

This one came up at our meeting.

One of the big ones. A deep one. That is, deep within. It causes so many other derivatives e.g. the inner and outer critic, grandiosity, paranoia, lack of self worth, hyper alertness...etc...fear: fear is a main source of many of our struggles.

I lived my life soaked with fear. It was my main driver. No one knew and would even think the opposite I hid it so well. So well I wouldn't admit it to myself. I spent my life trying to prove to myself that I wasn't riddled with fear. I did this by, for one, taking risks. But the fear was actually causing harm to my body both through my actions and through its presence, contorting my muscles and fascia and intestines....and continually dominating my neuron pathways and therefore my behavior, my relationships and relationship with the World.

I needed to recognise that I was a ball of fear. The first step: to accept that I had every right to be fearful. My child within, at my core, was full of fear and it be so. Then I started the work. That is the work and often pain of extracting the fear. Oh yes, overcoming the anger and resent at being made by the trauma of the abuse to be so fearful, and resent at having to take the responsibility for its expulsion. Accepting that no one, no group, no therapy, no book, despite being important tools, would take fear away for me: that is not an expression of an empty, lonely, hopeless 'oh nobody loves me, it's just not fair, oh woe is me, this is an selfish uncaring World'. No, it is empowerment. By taking responsibility I am reclaiming me and my life. With that, overcoming and accepting I can go into a life without fear. I can let it go. To, paradoxically, step by step see I don't need the fear anymore; fear has been part of my life, but I can let it go. To learn to let go of fear of a life without fear: to let go of fear of what may replace being fearful, to learn to welcome its replacement....accept that fearfulness and its derivatives have become a habit, a safety. To now embrace my change, to welcome the space that fear and its behavior leave, and to welcome that which fills that space.

Again, it is brutal self honesty that is the scalpel in this operation. The recognition of the fear is the first important incision.

It is consciously recognising all the myriad of behavioral traits spawned from fear, and consciously, time and time again until it becomes habit, recognise that space between the conscious you recognising them and doing them, and then choosing not to, choosing to let go instead. Experiencing that moment when you abseil for the first time, lean back and let the rope take your weight, that flinch of angst, and then recognising the relief that ensues. The relief that replaces. And you'll feel it's not new. It's been there all along, waiting for you.

It is body work. The fear is trapped in the body.

It is allowing yourself to find self time and peace... to stop and just be.

It is sharing and talking and speaking it out.

It is feeling that deep, deep, deep, deep fear...to sob & sob and feel so weak and vulnerable and to go with it and sit in it and let it come back again and again and again, well beyond what you think you can cope with and know that it will pass and that you are strong enough to let it pass through.

Trust me brothers, you will find an inner core. An inner core that is solid. It pulses. It will give you inner peace. And you can choose, whenever, to tip your head back and laugh, loudly, open mouthed at fear 'though silently within. Why? Because you have witnessed the worst of what fear can bring, and you have been through it. You will see clearly that your core, your soul, was simply stained with this fear. The fear wasn't you. That beautiful relentless soul that was the first thing of you when you took your very first breath has always been there. That is you, that pure and beautiful you that is always you. Fear is no match for that.

Fear is just an opportunity to strengthen by helping you feel at your most vulnerable. Know that fear is the shepherd of behavior for most people; they choose to escape their fear, never challenge it, and therefore allow it to dictate their lives. We are on a journey, an Odyssey, of recovery - it is a journey of discovery few choose, paying with a life half lived. We as survivors are equipped to deal with fear. Your little boy did, so can you: now you can dig it out and let it go. The time has come.

Love & Respect,

Greg.

Part of the diet of healing from trauma is well served by including the ingredient of helping others.

As mentioned: want to help yourself? Help others.

So, some way into my breakdown when I could risk going out of the flat, I enrolled as a volunteer with a couple of homeless centers. I found I could use my need for absolute control coupled with the energy of anger to be the cook at one place. This meant single handedly cooking for between 35 & 65 people such that the food was laid out at 1pm pretty much precisely, otherwise by 1:10pm at least one visitor would be moaning. The previous cook didn't turn up and when this came to light I happened to be buried in the kitchen doing something or other, the other two (we were short staffed) just backed out and left me to it. I evolved to resist 'help' (it wasn't), although opening all the 10 million tins (my hands ached) plus spreading margarine on all the slices of bread (everyone got at least three) was a drag. I know it was a tricky performance because from time to time I was asked to take in a person sent by their company to do a 'contribution' day. Invariably, they were highly educated young people working in 'The City' and were good at telling me how great they were, but nineteen times out of twenty they were useless and got in the way. Except on one occasion when a young chap, I say 'young' he was probably about thirty two, turned up. He was a married father and was 'in real life'. He had ideas about what we could do with the ingredients, consisting of random donations, and he wasn't daunted by firing up the giant ovens. For the first time I felt I could step back and let someone else take the wheel. I've looked back several times since and wondered what the trigger was. Was it that I was able to relax and let go? I can't say. I could analyze it but just now, and on reflection, I can't identify what set me off. I suspect if I were to be pushed for an answer I would only invent something, which is odd because typically I can pinpoint the moment that set me off, particularly given how the next hour or so unfolded.

I recall a feeling deep in my stomach, of nausea stretching in a band across my middle a little way below my rib cage to my groin. A feeling like I'd eaten something 'off'. My breathing became amplified, deliberate and shallow. I couldn't think. Things became echoed. My head filled with a mist. My throat locked. My intestines began to churn. Something was coming up. I recall the young man chatting to me, at me. I excused myself and left. I sat down away from people. Okay, something *was* coming up. This feeling had a different flavour to the time I was choking over the loo which began with nervous system convulsions, but I sensed it was big. It was going to be scary but I made the decision to go through it, right through it. Panic came, I recognized this: fear of suspected intense feelings, countered by expectation of challenge, matched with opportunity; I knew I had a chance to eject a lot of pain.

I thought about heading for the exit, I figured I had a small window of time to get home and get into bed, and perhaps be ready. But I knew if I left I could either fold half way and end up lying on the street, or divert the feeling by getting involved in the cycle ride on the busy road causing the sensation to go. But I knew it wouldn't be gone, rather back deep inside continuing to leak out as poisonous toxic behavior, self destruction, hopelessness and, and……and I would have diverted an opportunity to take a big step in my recovery.

I recall finding Geoff the manager. He had worked with the homeless for a long time and he had 'lived'. I knew he would sense my distress and be okay with it: he would cope. I don't recall what I said to him. I don't remember transmitting panic or being tearful, but he sensed my distress immediately. I knew he would. He was surrounded by other people and absorbed with something on the computer but he took one look into my eyes and stopped instantly, stood up and led me to an unfamiliar empty corridor; it was wide with no one about, and I folded. I lay on the ground in the fetal position and sobbed. I'm not just talking about sobbing, or even sobbing heavily, or even wailing. I'm talking about this deep, deep guttural yowling and convulsing from my guts. My face was contorted. I know because after awhile I felt my face severely aching, my facial muscles having been screwed up for so long.

It came up wave after wave after wave.

The pain. The pain. The pain. Ceaseless pain; and I knew it was fear. It was all the fear in me; all the fear locked in my body. I was the little boy night after night after night after night lying alone in fear: in the dead of night. Deep into the night when the rest of the World is asleep and no one is there, no one can hear you, no one knows, and no one cares: alone, shivering in fear. The hopelessness, the vulnerability, the defenselessness, my teddies stacked on the edge of the bed to protect me. This was me. This was what had happened to me. This is what had happened to me as a little boy. The realization of this. Realising it. That is: going through it, that fear, the fear of the before, the waiting, the anticipation, the listening for the floor boards, every creak making my heart freeze and then pound with fear.

I felt Geoff's presence. Even he, I suspect, had not witnessed anything quite the same but he was well equipped to accept it; during my tenure at the centre we had witnessed and dissolved some extreme behavior, probably shocking to many an office worker. I knew what it was when it came through me. All that fear: gallons of it. But I squeezed and squeezed and rode it out. I want this fear out. I want it gone. I dug right in. I really dug in. I invited it up. I challenged it. I stayed with it. This was pure healing. It would pass.

Geoff murmured after a while and I nodded, signaling he could leave: I'd be okay, it was subsiding. I lay in it for an age. Lying in this semi lit corridor until eventually I became conscious of the industrial carpet pressed into my cheek and a surreal view of an unremarkable corridor.

I rolled onto my back. 'Ooowwweee, feerrrkkinn 'ell,' I said. I'd done it. I was through it. I had emptied the bulk of the fear out. I even gave a wry smile. I knew I was going to feel different now on. I knew I was going to be different. Whatever life dealt up from now on it wouldn't matter. And I wouldn't worry what that might be. I could do it.

I don't remember going home, I just remember being exhausted. I later felt intense resent when I realized how much fear I'd been carrying and later, until just very recently, anger often possessed me, anger at being made to experience so much fear when I was a boy, and having to go through it again. But now I felt different. I felt good.

I used to despise the fear in me, subsequently spending my life numbing out, or challenging myself by being reckless, or contrarily evoking angst by worrying that I was a fraud, worrying that I'd be 'found out', feeling that I was loaded with fear and would be found wanting at some critical moment when it mattered.

My voice has changed. I can choose to speak directly from a calm solid source deep within. I do concern myself with the future, looking to the horizon for possibilities as is sensible but I don't catastrophise, knowing whatever comes I'll cope. An inner wholeness I previously sensed some have, probably the only feature of some others I've ever truly envied, I now have. You can have this too.

After India and the loo incident, I arrived back in Sydney and took up a fast lane job and blow torched the candle at both ends and, coupled with imploding anger, I wound up with a duodenal ulcer. I had a barium meal which sets like concrete and I recall the feeling of being solid inside rather than having the sensation that my guts had rotted. After the corridor incident, I felt like I had swallowed a barium meal. I felt like I was operating from a feeling of being stable rather than tipping off balance. I could look people in the eye. For awhile I worried that all fear had gone as I found myself casually walking across busy roads, lifting up a hand and getting cars to slow down. I actually crossed Fulham Palace Road and walked in front of stationary truck, and a motorbike coming up on the inside nearly hit me so I decided this crossing the road when it suited me business had gone far enough [fear has a purpose]. I endured IBS most of life (only absent when I was smoking weed dipped in heroine, which it can be by way of getting you seriously addicted, fashionable in Sydney back in the 80's & the go to relish of one ex-dealer ex-'friend' in the UK - the opiate serving to clog me up), but IBS went overnight never to return. Now I get the opposite (yes alright mate, we get your drift thank you).

Fear and angst are locked into the body, in the gut & in the shoulders (in my experience). Fear creates tension causing the shoulders to flinch and pull the shoulder blades up such that the neck is protected from attack. It is natural to tense up the muscles in order to protect the neck. My posture changed. I began to occupy my space.

Not all the fear had gone but the exiting bulk from my gut liberated me. I became more me. I would no longer have to make an excuse to be me, or wear a mask of a persona in order to feel safe. I was okay being me, at last. I wasn't hyper vigilant anymore. It was soon after I had the tube experience where someone fell on me. I intuited people felt more comfortable around me. But sometime later I dealt to a couple of knots I had in my upper back. As I got into them I could trace their origin i.e. I was able to pick how my body was flinching and holding tension in my back, and I was able to feel what thoughts and feelings created this flinching, also able to experience and process the trapped feelings on their release (as described). It has taken over a year of stretching nearly every evening to get into these knots. They are bound into the fascia. It takes persistence. But now my physiology has changed.

The quest of recovery gifted authenticity.

Fear has a habit of presenting unnecessary roadblocks re-directing you from your path. We often conform to these roadblocks without question. Fear buried inside bleeds into your life, and we add to our fear reserves as we travel. We are adept at this cycle of obeying and restocking, always maintaining fear as a primary guide. It is fear the media and politicians use with considerable success to garner attention, manipulate, and fuel our fear tank. People do it to each other. But the entity that most propels fear in you, is you. When facing into fears, even little by little, you will find they are just holograms. You turn back into them and you pass through them *('though not a moving motorcycle!)*

Recovery means change and flexibility. Change requires growth and pain. Growth means strength.

If you do not turn into feelings and experience them, but choose instead to medicate or divert, they will forever haunt you and own you. You will forever forfeit your freedom.

You have a choice over how you expend the rest of your precious short life. You can allow triggers and fears to control and own you, or ***you*** can decide to free yourself.

3. Anger

Anger is a big one for me. Anger, threatening to tip over into violence then imploding; feeling like a danger to myself and others. Worrying, especially when the Tsunami of the breakdown hit, when I wasn't crumpled with sorrow but pacing about growling with body boiling rage, closed peripheral vision, bile pulsing into my throat projecting venomous adrenaline from my stomach up the back of my neck filling my head and threatening to squirt from my saliva glands and tear ducts whilst I hissed like a cornered cat; worry that on becoming conscious, after the mist had cleared, that I'd look down at bodies covered in blood. Anger often consumed me in the past and typically I would be alone when it happened, but during my breakdown and recovery it was essential I was alone when the anger came.

The anger needs to be expressed. There may well be a lot of it. ('expressed' appropriately).

During an afternoon session at the weekend with the brothers we spilt into smaller groups and I claimed I had run out of things to say, to which the facilitator responded 'I doubt that'. Anyhow, I tried the 'bash the punch bag' option, rather than sitting down and discussing an issue, but wondered if I needed to because I was feeling calm. Come my turn I got hold of the pick axe handle and a short while later after the red mist had cleared I was gasping for breath and my arms ached. That was over two years ago. My anger attacks are less frequent and less intense and often need inviting up by me: there is still a lot of anger but it is not repressed or buried and festering, it is just nicely resting in its kennel. My first therapist identified that I was going around with a big dangerous dog in front of me on a leash and I used this dog to protect me by keeping people away. If they got too close the dog would growl. It was useful to objectify the anger; I could view it, make decisions as to what to do with it equipped with an objective awareness. I could step away from the anger, see it as a thing. I went on step by step to move the dog alongside me instead of prowling in front, then behind me, then into the kennel, and finally fast asleep inside. I've always got him but he is where he needs to be, mostly, and notably, asleep rather than pacing around snarling in a pen.

Trauma survivors often have 'anger issues'. Survivors, understandably, often possess a lot of anger and are unsure how to express it, prone to excess or repression causing implosion. I was like that. Expression of my anger (or any other emotions for that matter) was prohibited. Anger is a normal and natural emotion everybody has, and trauma survivors often have every right to be angry. But expression of anger in appropriate ways has, in part, to be learnt.

Unexpressed anger can be harmful, as can inappropriately expressed anger. Unexpressed anger will implode and has negative effect. I understand that depression can be or is, I'm not sure which, imploded anger. This explains a lot to me. I have endured repeated bouts of depression, but as part of my recovery I have been processing and discharging a lot of anger, like a lot a lot, and I don't get depressed anymore. I get sad but I don't get depressed. Work on one thing and another fades.

Let me drift off topic a bit here, if I may, from anger to depression and subsequently differentiating sadness from depression. In essence, I would say depression hangs about for a long time, whereas sadness I find, at most, lasts for a few days, and it doesn't dig in so deep. I can still function and the hiss of the suicide snake can't be heard. Now I'm quite happy to be sad (eh?). I can sit in it knowing it will pass. I understand that being sad is perfectly normal and being a bit arty I use sadness to access other shades of feelings I am getting more familiar with, melancholy for example. Being sad and being with the sadness is being alive. It is being close to oneself and gives me empathy for others, and therefore connection. Going around believing you are entitled to be happy all the time is not aligned with reality. Sadness is going to happen; so life is going to be easier if you embrace it and ask, 'what is this sadness teaching me?' But not to immerse in it permanently, there is a line. Where is that line? The line of paradox: sitting in sadness, being with it, experiencing it and going through it (emotions pass – all of them no matter how powerful), verses wallowing i.e. choosing to expand the sadness, sustaining and inflicting it on others by going beyond sharing into the realms of 'dumping on people', therefore spreading abuse.

Imploded anger results in negative physiological effects, a probable major ingredient of my ulcer of years ago: the stomach grinding, the unreasonable behavior, all being anger leaking out destructively; hyper criticism, irritability, multiple jobs, life threatening recklessness, addiction to drugs (suppression), workaholic, etc, etc, a lot of my life was driven by anger. I used anger to prevent people getting close and seeing how vulnerable and frightened I was. Anger can be a mask for fear.

When I recognized how angry I was and process it I became a lot calmer but worried its absence would leave me vulnerable to being a victim, without an angry vibe people would take advantage of me, and I was concerned it might unplug the force motivating me to get stuff done. Again, I feared the 'perceived' void that would replace it and further, I feared what might fill it. Also, a big part for me was recognizing I was addicted to being angry. Being angry felt empowering. But really...living a life invariably tainted with anger? It had to go. But there is an odd experience of grief for its loss, or more accurately, a loss of its excess. Plus a fear, as outlined before, of a 'letting go' of an old tool for survival and a fear of what will replace it, a fear of a perceived unknown: a fear of change.

Anger needs to be expelled but, by its very nature, this is best done in a controlled environment; punch the punch bag, shoot at the range, throttle the cushion…

I've discussed anger at length with a few survivors of childhood trauma. Evidently it will return over and over especially in the early stages of recovery from trauma. I am just about shedding the last remnants of excess anger some five and half years after the Tsunami of my breakdown. But let's be clear, anger is a useful, natural emotion: if you read this book and find it useful and of value, we have my anger to thank, I am using it as a driver. The expression of anger in all its glory at an injustice is a beautiful force. I am very, very, very angry (massive under statement) about the abuse of children, and I am using this anger to do something about it. If I can help survivors get off the back foot in life, get beyond 'getting by' and help get them on to the front foot, then they/ you may choose to join in the fray to stop childhood abuse.

So, on a pragmatic level, down to basics: at the weekend with the brothers we smashed the punch bag with the pick axe handle one by one whilst others watched and shouted their support. It was a great release, both the watching and doing. Before this event, for about two years as part of my recovery I held a cushion daily and throttled to death the abusers i.e. focusing purely on the childhood abusers. By default, all those I added to the long list of people who'd 'done me a wrong' over the years I'd promised myself 'I would get to' (but never would, I would just harbor more internal pain manifested, ultimately, as knotted muscles, tight fascia, and perhaps depression etc) seemed to dissipate. Throttling the cushion is something I could do in a controlled fashion on my own. I found I could do it like a regular exercise at a regular time. I didn't have to feel angry before I did it. I would simply grasp the cushion and easily think myself into the anger via the abuse and up it would come, wave after wave. One thing I would say though, if you do use this technique then flex and stretch your hands first - I put so much pressure through mine I sprained them and for days, it hurt to even pick up a mug of coffee (a 'how to knock a nail in' piece of advice).

I personally think aiming to live in a trance like harmony floating in 'at one with the World' calmness is a load of nonsense. Alright for the bloke with the shaved head wearing orange pajamas listening to gongs up the mountain (all expenses paid), but ask the single parent pushing a pram containing a screaming two year old with a full nappy and a three year old careening towards the traffic on a scooter followed by the yapping dog, to empty their mind of thoughts about getting food and paying the bills. Really? They're in the real World with no room for such indulgence. Few of us have. Okay, good to take a leaf out the 'guru's book and get into relaxation, its vital, but everyday living means irritability and anger will get created, they will project out, or be internalized.

Trauma generates a big ball of anger which lodges inside; further anger will therefore be added to it, often creating an overreaction or a deeper implosion to everyday events. We need to dislodge and expel the held ball of anger.

Also, critically, remember the stuff about 'space' and driving? With self awareness we can anticipate situations that might make us angry and choose to interject space and find another way of being, at least soften the level of anger to an everyday situation. And again, create a new better way of being (top down).

The other thing/s is to ask, 'why does this type of situation/event/comment make me so angry?' 'Why does this anger keep coming up/occurring?' 'What am I avoiding/in denial about?/not facing into?' 'Am I being triggered?' 'What is it and why?'

Why was I so excessively impatient? Was it something to do with waiting outside the school, which we lived a long way from when I was six, and all the other children had gone home? Even all the children from the big school down the road who got out later had gone by, but they didn't see me as I used to hide back inside the gates because I was afraid of them. Finally, the mother would turn up and find me sitting alone in the street. She had been chatting with someone and figured I could wait, if she even managed to think about me at all. Later I realized she did that with everyone. Other people didn't really matter very much. It was 'her', they could wait.

... and 'why was I so irritable?' The output of a trauma survivor is often irritability: a transmission of an energy sourced from inner turmoil, giving the survivor influence and a sense of control over their environment by affecting it. Was my irritability added to because the mother taught young children as a job and after getting me home she made me stay outside the house whilst she rested, and any

attempt at interaction by me was met with irritability: stay away. I irritated her, so going forward, other people irritated me.

What I am asking is: what is it that keeps you repeating the same pattern of anger, of shame, of guilt, and others? What are the 'triggers' and what has created them? And moreover, what are you going to do about them? Moan or change?

'I'm stuck. Can't get through it. Can't get past it. Can't get over it. Can't understand it away. Can't get it out. I've tried I really have. What do I do?..'

…it's okay….let it be, maybe try working on something else….you'll wonder later why you were so obsessed….[see: huffing and puffing]

Communicating with other trauma survivors confirms a feature I found in terms of working on stuff. Sometimes resolving an issue may feel like chipping at a granite wall. You try everything; writing about it, talking about it, reading about it, digging right into it, but it won't shift. No problem: let it be. Let it drift. Focus on something else. One day someone will be talking about the very issue you were so bothered about, but you'll notice it has now dissipated. Yes, you can isolate anger or shame and deal with them, but the processing of exaggerated feelings that don't serve you is imprecise. Rather like steering a boat verses steering a car. You turn the steering wheel of a car and it changes direction immediately, not so a boat, there is a lag between turning the wheel and a change of direction. If you understand why you are repeating a behavior and desire change, but still keep reacting the same way, it's okay; it takes time to change direction, to take on new patterns of emotional behavior.

Another feature to consider is: this is how I am. I have a personality, this is my nature and I am okay with that, hence the irony of the joke about Bob in the pub. We ain't blokes sitting around all day humming in caves, we've got lives to live and that can often press our buttons. Getting okay with your self is a big indicator and measure of recovery. Being okay being who you are with all your flaws, and being with everybody else and all theirs. And beyond that, celebrating those flaws: Kintsugi.

4. Shame (& Guilt)

These are a couple of insidious feelings that curl around you and suffocate. They are tricky to pin down in any way. They can drop over you like mist and linger unabating. They can speak with hushed clarity and undermine you in a subtle but powerful ways. You can feel like you are wading through sludge until you slow down and stop and submit. They can alter their volume, drown out everything then become a continuous whisper. They'll haunt, finding sustenance in different ways.

They are a poison that seeps into you. But, for poisons there are antidotes, Shame & Guilt are no exceptions.

Let's detach the two. Shame is about the self; a negative feeling the 'self' bestows because of a low opinion of oneself. Guilt is a negative feeling created because of an external i.e. a feeling of responsibility for an effect one has had. Shame is how the person perceives themselves and will be perceived: their persona. Guilt is a feeling in response to an action. I am more focused on dealing with shame, which is often debilitating and inflated in survivors causing self-sabotaging behavior.

Trauma survivors often carry shame. They often feel the trauma is somehow their fault, that they are to blame. That they are guilty of an action and as such, deserve shame. WRONG.

The problem with shame is that we all naturally try i.e. engage conscious effort, to turn away from it which conversely causes friction thereby enhancing the effects. And contrarily, if we carry shame we keep going back to re-expose ourselves to it. It is a 'push me pull me' effect, rather like it is stuck to you with gooey glue. But let's be clear: shame and guilt are natural; we are supposed to feel them. The problem arises when shame and guilt become a way of being i.e. an almost permanent state, rather than either or both passing by as they should.

I believe continuously questioning why I am feeling shameful when it strikes i.e. digging around each time and trying to find where shame has made its den and rooting it out is going to be too absorbing and complicated. Shame will writhe around changing its guise too easily, it is too tricky to repeatedly get to grips with and decode. I think beating shame and likewise guilt, takes a simple combination of consciously employing the habit of avoidance. Plus, I constantly catapult in fiercely burning lumps of self acceptance and self compassion which destroy shame: the siege approach. That way in time the two of them get starved out. I don't feed them by sitting in them too much.

The trick with shame and guilt is to accept they are natural and have a purpose and allow for some i.e. give them a place which, conversely, causes shrinkage. And I marry this acceptance with the decision that feeling excessive shame and guilt is going to stop. Just a sniff of shame is enough, no need to keep inhaling which is what it wants. Decision made. And by way of reinforcement get a mantra going that you can chant to yourself.

'It was not my fault'. 'I am not to blame.' 'It was the abuser's responsibility, not mine.'

'I am a wonderful human being, just right as I am. I am doing just great.'

Be clear about your mantra because shame is going to be trying on its charm first chance it gets.

A pesticide you can spray on shame is self worth. Shame is not much use in the face of self worth, and trauma survivors need to keep pumping it up. Those of us raised in abusive neglectful households, especially, need to regularly work at self worth as if an exercise programme, along with your physical exercise programme (also a good way of developing self worth).

Self care, self love, self worth and self compassion all take conscious work. Keep working at the self worth and shame will find little to attach itself too.

Feeling shameful? Make a decision. Go and do something positive for you.......

Contradicting the avoidance strategy, another weapon of choice to shrink shame is to consciously investigate and recognize where it is coming from, which may need professional help, and not necessarily when it strikes i.e. investigate objectively. But I hasten to add, 'investigate, not 're-re-investigate', i.e. do once and have done with. Why is our shame being exaggerated? By digging into the past we can see if shame was attached to us in childhood. Was shame used as a control? Or absorbed from the abuser? People project their shame onto others by way of trying to shed it; the hot potato. And festering shame will turn into other abusive energies like envy. People feel shameful and begin to envy those that outwardly don't carry shame. The parents deliberately paid no interest in my adult life because I escaped them, and so went on to envy me for not having to flounder in the shame they felt.

I lived in the middle east when I was twenty two. I took a one way ticket in 1985 when only the hyper wealthy stayed on a plane for more than three hours, and few people were Muslim in the UK. People told me I would watch hangings every weekend and folk getting their hands chopped off in the street; I would end up in a hut in the desert with no passport and would struggle to ever get back. 'They' being bright educated people 'told' me whilst looking me in the eye earnestly. 'They' knew what was going to happen to me, because they needed to project their fear onto me (in the same way people project shame onto others). Their reason i.e. their excuse, was they were trying to warn me.

I was cleansed of their fears on the first morning when I was nearly ran over by a car – no one warned me they drove on the opposite side.
Genuine practical advice based on lived experience is invaluable.

Find the sources of shame and of guilt and evaporate them with the light of understanding. It's not yours, it doesn't belong to you anymore, let go. It belongs to someone else. Turn into and face it and sit in it. And next time the remnants of shame slides towards you stamp on it, and consciously fill yourself with self worth.

The survivor not choosing to recover will find ways of distributing the abuse they endured. For example, being an addict, by way of escaping, is abusive to those around you. An addict puts their addiction first; they will say they don't but they do, the addiction owns their soul and therefore their morality. The journey of healing will involve traversing and processing the rough terrain of facing into behavior created by the trauma: behavior which, in turn, fashions guilt and shame. Note: there is a school of thought advocating the trauma survivor had no control over their behavior and therefore should feel no guilt for it, and therefore has no need to make amends. I'm not so sure. I am of the opinion that once a person begins the journey of recovery and becomes aware of behavior abusive to others but doesn't choose to change, they are being irresponsible. This is irresponsibility hiding behind trauma: trauma is being used as an excuse. And let's be clear, it is often irresponsibility of some that causes trauma to others, especially to children. Behaving irresponsibly by using trauma as an excuse is perpetuating abuse. Being abusive is not healing.

Making amends is a good way to address destructive behavior and resolve associated shame and guilt, and is therefore healing. For one, making amends makes the survivor truly recognize the behavior, thereby clicking the ratchet of healing. And importantly, making amends gives those affected by the behavior understanding which prompts their forgiveness and acknowledgement of the survivor's journey, all further serving to contribute to the survivor's recovery.

Making amends takes courage, is not always easy and doesn't always get the response the survivor expects or hopes for, but even via application alone, regardless of responses, the survivor moves forward.

I personally found making amends to be a valuable process. It taught me to scrutinize my behavior, my effect on others and be totally honest with myself. The open conscious declaration of any abusive behavior on my part helped me to acknowledge and neutralize it: consciously separating me from its pattern, leading to conquering my addiction to illicit drugs. It taught me a new behavioral procedure: that of replacing irresponsibility with accountability.

Making amends helped cleanse me. The confessional aspect wiped the slate and gave me a fresh start with myself and those around me on which I could build, in turn helping to diminish feelings of shame which were holding back my recovery. I also felt it propelled the campaign of growing my self worth: the act of being open and honest: enacting the courage to make amends.

Confessing my sins brought me closer to others by healing wounds and therefore took away barriers of distrust and masks, bringing me closer to humanity. Plus, I was humbled by the forgiveness I received which inspired forgiveness for others within me. They forgave and understood and recognized they could not judge, and witnessing and being the recipient of that was a humbling lesson, and with that I grew.

Therein lays the path of the evolving, responsible, accountable adult.

There was a price however. I saw so clearly others, all sorts, stuck in often destructive behavioral patterns divorcing them from close relationships; from truly being themselves and living an authentic life, and not necessarily trauma survivors. I had to choose and still do; to go along with their patterns and be the 'me' that fitted around them. There is the temptation to call them out and righteously expose them. There is the temptation to put the old mask back on and go along at the cost of my integrity. There is the temptation to drop them at the cost of throwing the baby out with the bath water, because there is still good in there. My view is if they are likely to bring back negative habits, for example hanging around addicts, they've got to go. Otherwise, being flexible is part of the thriver's package. In terms of going along with stuff I don't support e.g. language that no longer aligns with my values I am now equipped with 'No', and I simply keep those folk from my own inner sanctum.

When one searches for and finds their own truth, the price is seeing the self deception of others.

5. Grief

.....is a massive one too.

Be sure, grief is an emotion the trauma survivor will experience as part of the recovery journey. There will be major bouts of grief which can be physically crippling. When grief hits it can bring you to your knees. I recall buckling and collapsing in a shower, curled up for an age in the square well, sobbing and sobbing. Grief will strike us all at some point in our lives: impossible to escape. To experience grief is very natural and a right of passage. I remember a documentary about the effects of the Lockerbie bombings on the families of the victims. Suse Lowenstein, whose son died in the bombing, created 76 sculptures of women depicting the moment when they heard their loved one had been killed. They show exquisitely the powerful physical effect, among others, grief can have when it strikes (Dark Elegy).

Grief affects us all differently. It can knock us down on the spot or hang for an age making us feel heavy and depressed, then keep coming back in waves when we are not expecting it triggered by even a waft of a scent. I recall sometime after Rich took his life I was thinking about him whilst climbing just three flights of stairs and having to stop at the top bent over, my legs exhausted and short of breath, my heart pounding, feeling like I'd carried a sack of bricks on my back. I actually stood bent over at the top holding the rail: the weight of the grief.

Grief is typically only associated with death, but it can strike for a variety of losses. On the journey of recovery from trauma, grief will visit, perhaps regularly. I grieved for me as a little boy, and I grieved for the loss of the ideal of my childhood I had painted in my mind, had been sold by the 'parents', that I was 'lucky' and should be quiet and grateful. To see children happily playing would often, until recently, trigger grief: grief for the loss of an innocent childhood: grief for all abused children. I also found I resented me as a small boy because his/my emergence brought guilt for having ignored his loneliness and pain. I viewed him as a weakness within me that I had been desperately avoiding all my life, and I grieved when I realized this. But he was me. And he was the strong one, and together we felt the grief and pain and became whole.

There were a multitude of other moments and periods of grief. It was deep grief I encountered, I now realize, when I lay in bed every afternoon incapacitated during my breakdown. I have grieved when people close had died, but never before had it been with me so long or been so intense. I wondered if it would ever end. Somewhere in the midst of this my life long friend Mark, my childhood escape, died suddenly. That was the second time I called my first therapist. The grief became unbearable. I felt like I'd had my time and everything was shutting down and being taken away from me, as though smothered in a thick slab of concrete, unable to breathe.

I believe the key is that grief needs to be experienced and needs to pass through. And it will. It will take longer than you want. You can expect that. Grief wounds but heals leaving scars that open up from time to time.

Recovery brings a need for a lot of 'letting go', it is a major requirement of recovery because one must change; to change one has to let stuff go, and when letting go there is likely to be grief. Grief you wouldn't have imagined will be there. Expect to be surprised how grief will come and possess you even, for example, when you let behaviors go that no longer serve you.

The one major route to expressing grief is to sob. Talking, sharing, writing, listening, they all help, but the best way is to sob. We are designed to sob. I'm not just talking about crying. I'm talking about body shaking, face contorting, gasping and wailing: tears and snot. If it comes, get it out. Never mind the 'English way' of holding it back and keeping in control and stiff upper lip, and all that bollocks, which is the approach that got so many poor souls 'shell shock' (trauma): imploded fear and grief.

Experience the pain of the grief or pay the price of the pain continuing, never leaving, coming back and back, re-wounding you and never allowing you to be free. Know that when you are in pain, when grief comes up and you truly experience it and go through it, you are growing.

Grief is part of life. It is part of being a human. A large part of recovery is about experiencing grief. Grief is very personal. It is different for everybody in the way it strikes, when, where, why and how it affects you. It may come disguised as depression or anger. But look and feel again, it may be grief. That way you can understand it and accept it and feel it.

The gift of grief is that it brings you empathy for what others experience. It brings you closer to humanity. And it brings truth.

It gifts the truth of you, your authenticity.

Survival

I have a theory about recovery from trauma which may be contentious. It may be an already held belief.

As a survivor of childhood trauma I lacked safety as a child. The feeling of safety was taken away from me. Safety, as I said before, is vital to humans and vital to our development. We seek safety first. By way of experiencing safety, trauma survivors often create mechanisms, defenses; often over compensating with behavior that works for them during their lives, even though it may be destructive.

My personal arsenal of safety mechanisms is considerable; having a temper, transmitting I have a temper, being hyper critical of the outside World (skeptical), acerbic wit, big blustering ego, compartmentalizing (that is separating events, people, things, thoughts), workaholic, freeze people out, charm etc, etc, etc all by way of maintaining control of my environment in order to gain perceived safety. Once aware of such behaviors and linked to the cause, it is easy to see the same in others. Some trauma survivors will implode and self destruct, whilst others, including me (at times), will sometimes be seen as successful because they have this ability to shut off from their feelings and maintain what is often viewed as strength. Trauma survivors are often good at handling traumas, able to stay calm and act in a crisis, able to disassociate.

I am of the belief that yes, negative behavioral pathways can be diluted, but can they be disposed of? Can we hope to dispose of them? What amount of effort is involved?

Perhaps we can utilize these well honed skills that have served us in the past, to some extent, and re-deploy them?

During my recovery I became aware of a personality trait e.g. the ability to switch personas (masks). I attempted to separate myself from this behavior to observe and be aware of it, so I might discard it.
Note: the childhood trauma survivor learns not to express their pain, stifled by threats, shame etc. To get by they must 'wear masks' so as to be accepted and also hide their inner pain. Some have to project an acceptable demeanor e.g. quiet gratitude, so as to minimize danger in a household where abuse is perpetrated. But is it necessary or possible to completely discard a pattern of being. People do change, I have, but surely some traits could prove useful for recovery? For example, conditioned to detach from feelings, having only an 'on/off' switch, aided my survival and enabled me to weather the storms of life, but via the journey of recovery I could see this 'all or nothing thinking' meant I was missing out the many shades in between, but I have used that ruthlessness to help me recover.

Many survivors of trauma often see things only in black and white (not literally), as A or B, with no grey in between. I employed that simplification to stop me from buying drugs. I gave myself a strict choice when it came to drugs, I either bought them or I didn't anymore. I know addiction could easily renegotiate with me if armed only with the deterrent of a woolly list of 'reasons why I shouldn't'. And moderation can be harder than abstinence. Similarly, I used the same A or B thinking on recovery: 'Yes' I will recover, and 'No' to suicide. The decision is the absolute: it is the rule. I use the same A or B with shame. I'm done with shame. I felt it through; I get it, so now I just sense it then jump on it. Yes, I can choose to either feel it right through and let it pass, or not bother with it much; I now choose the latter.

Survivors of childhood abuse lost the control of themselves even if momentarily, control was taken away from them. They often have a need to compensate and devise mechanisms to gain control as they pass through life. Grasping the concept that the World is full of uncertainty I have no control over, although I was always trying to, was difficult for me; and in the same vein recognizing that my frustration with life, and feeling I was on the wrong planet, all stemmed from being a survivor came as a revelation. So, with the onslaught of my breakdown I made the *decision to recover.* I took this need for control and used to it pull me through recovery. I marshaled myself. Instead of trying to control the World, I took to controlling what I could control. One element of which was my health. I took to a routine of getting up at the same time every day and exercising, whether I liked it or not. I coupled the need for control with its partner the need for routine, which previously I applied to ritualistic drug abuse, into other positives like doing the 12 steps, round and round, going to the meetings, keeping a journal, self care….

As a trauma survivor you may well have developed all sorts of survival mechanisms. They have probably contributed to how you so courageously got this far. Consider that a lot of recovery is about reframing stuff i.e. looking at the same things through a different lens, changing the context. Your survival mechanisms may now be proving, or have proved, to be net destructive ('net': I mean the balance of behavior against result/s) and you may now feel it's time for a review, but there may be positive uses for those mechanisms. Maybe it is useful to re-frame them, redirect them. Recovery, followed closely by developing resilience, is about attaining flexible thinking. Rigid thinking is often a mechanism of survivors (again, back to the need for safety hence: 'this is this' and 'this is that', no argument, the end – viewing things in absolutes makes them identifiable, easy to collate, understandable and less threatening) which can conversely be re-deployed to other aspects of life, e.g. being rigid about stopping self criticism…! And bounce the inner self critic into another role, like looking at your diet!

Now, how can I use this ice skate?

What I am saying is: you can't just stop being you even if you want to. I know you may desperately want to at times. Change doesn't necessarily mean stopping rather, perhaps, redirecting.

And here's an additional tool / philosophy / approach that ***'you should'*** adopt [that's right – right between the eyes] if you don't already, over and above all others …….gratitude.

Every night after the news of the tumour my wife and I lay in bed thinking of things to be grateful for. They were always there. And seeking gratitude became a habit.

BTW – we decided not to have any more treatment and stick to the health and smoothie routine. The latest news is that the tumour has 'arrested and retracted' – Love + Will = powerful force.

The tumour taught us to embrace and appreciate life, and taught us that we can overcome anything. To be present, and appreciate, and be grateful.

Before I go (actually shut up – temporarily at least), I want to add in two more bits, both of which deserve a book at least.

Forgiveness: I mentioned earlier a doctor said I needed to forgive, like I needed to forgive in order to evolve and prevent being stuck with the suffering. Once I forgave all would be well. I'd be fine. I'd be happy, all the time.

I need to stress here very clearly: when it comes to forgiveness, of all subjects involved in recovery, it is my firm belief that it needs to have your fingerprint on it. How you do or don't forgive (applying your definition) is up to you and you alone.

As mentioned, some of my responses to questions in the 12 steps stayed the same. Forgiveness was one of them i.e. they were short, Anglo Saxon and very dismissive. The idea of 'forgiveness' made my blood boil. It gets complicated, but my survival and recovery depended upon defiance and revenge to a large extent, and therefore forgiveness conflicted with these energies. So 'forgiveness' was not for me. But I later found I was obsessing about a handful of related viewpoints and figured if thinking about 'forgiveness' was often creating a net result of imploded anger i.e. continuing an effect of trauma, then I should take a look. I knew I needed to accept in order to recover, but I thought acceptance and forgiveness were bonded. In my mind if I accept I therefore, by default, forgive. And I would not, by my definition of 'forgiveness', be letting any through. I was stuck.

This pattern became dislodged when I took on board the concept of 'living alongside' the abuse, as my first therapist wisely proposed.

The abuse is there, almost as an addition rather than an 'all'; now I could step away from it and view it. So, 'living alongside' helped me to *accept* that I am a CSA (trauma) survivor; in effect creating another rail of thought I could travel along and therefore move past 'forgiveness' which now had space around it and wasn't blocking progress e.g. making me angry. Forgiveness and acceptance were de-coupled. I could now put the *acceptance* piece in the puzzle in its own place.

The abuse and trauma is not the whole of me. It does not define me.

I later went on to 'forgive' that childhood sexual abuse happened to me. 'It' (Childhood Abuse) is an 'is' – very sadly it happens with alarming frequency on a scale that needs to be put at the forefront of the consciousness of every society – and it happened to me. It doesn't make it right. I don't therefore forgive the existence of CSA. I only forgive that it happened to me. That way I can accept that it happened and then do something about it. Like Oscar the meditation teacher said to me back in '87, 'if I accept something, then I can deal with it.'

I do not however, forgive the abusers. I understand they were mentally ill. But that is not a reason to forgive, according to my thinking just now.

Trust: is a massive topic for survivors of abuse. Abuse violates and destroys trust. There is no set line when it comes to establishing trust. It moves for us all, is different for us all, and changes with time. In my life I have wavered between being completely trusting and the pole opposite with no in between which can easily lead to disappointment, disconnection and isolation. I have very good reason not to trust. It has taken a lot of work to build trust. I have learnt to take it step by step. Building trust, I have gathered, takes time and faith, and comes with risk. Group work helped me a lot; to share deep issues without judgment or tariff. And step by step I discovered I could share more about how I felt with people around me, and in return they shared with me. Building trust takes work. But it is not to be shied away from. To learn to trust is an essential element to enjoying the Eden of recovery. To live without trust, I have learnt is…well…if you don't stop and stick your nose in the flower and inhale, you will never know.

Summary

There is no summary. This journey of recovery and discovery is on going. I & you & all are a work in progress, so let's keep moving and evolving.

One day you'll wonder what that noise is, it will be familiar you've heard it before, and then you'll realize, it's you laughing!

God grant me the serenity to accept the things I cannot change,
The courage too change the things I can,
And the wisdom to know the difference.

The Serenity Prayer

Regardless of your religious or non-religious beliefs….still a great mantra.

You can do this.

Love does conquer all.

contact author: improvsax@email.com

Printed in Great Britain
by Amazon

70822545R00149